New Directions for
Adult and Continuing
Education

Susan Imel
Jovita M. Ross-Gordon
Joellen E. Coryell
COEDITORS-IN-CHIEF

Contexts, Practices and Challenges: Critical Insights from Continuing Professional Education

Maureen Coady

EDITOR

Number 151 • Fall 2016
Jossey-Bass
San Francisco

Contexts, Practices and Challenges: Critical Insights from Continuing Professional Education
Maureen Coady (ed.)
New Directions for Adult and Continuing Education, no. 151
Susan Imel, Jovita M. Ross-Gordon, and Joellen E. Coryell Coeditors-in-Chief

Microfilm copies of issues and articles are available in 16mm and 35mm, as well as microfiche in 105mm, through University Microfilms Inc., 300 North Zeeb Road, Ann Arbor, Michigan 48106-1346.

NEW DIRECTIONS FOR ADULT AND CONTINUING EDUCATION (ISSN 1052-2891, electronic ISSN 1536-0717) is part of The Jossey-Bass Higher and Adult Education Series and is published quarterly by Wiley Subscription Services, Inc., A Wiley Company, at Jossey-Bass, One Montgomery Street, Suite 1200, San Francisco, CA 94104-4594. POSTMASTER: Send address changes to New Directions for Adult and Continuing Education, Jossey-Bass, One Montgomery Street, Suite 1200, San Francisco, CA 94104-4594.

New Directions for Adult and Continuing Education is indexed in CIJE: Current Index to Journals in Education (ERIC); Contents Pages in Education (T&F); ERIC Database (Education Resources Information Center); Higher Education Abstracts (Claremont Graduate University); and Sociological Abstracts (CSA/CIG).

INDIVIDUAL SUBSCRIPTION RATE (in USD): $89 per year US/Can/Mex, $113 rest of world; institutional subscription rate: $335 US, $375 Can/Mex, $409 rest of world. Single copy rate: $29. Electronic only–all regions: $89 individual, $335 institutional; Print & Electronic–US: $98 individual, $402 institutional; Print & Electronic–Canada/Mexico: $98 individual, $442 institutional; Print & Electronic–Rest of World: $122 individual, $476 institutional.

EDITORIAL CORRESPONDENCE should be sent to the Coeditors-in-Chief, Susan Imel, 3076 Woodbine Place, Columbus, Ohio 43202-1341, e-mail: imel.1@osu.edu; or Jovita M. Ross-Gordon, Texas State University, CLAS Dept., 601 University Drive, San Marcos, TX 78666; Joellen E. Coryell, Texas State University, 601 University Drive, ASBS Room 326 San Marcos, TX 78666-4616.

Cover design: Wiley
Cover Images: © Lava 4 images | Shutterstock

www.josseybass.com

CONTENTS

EDITOR'S NOTES

Given the increasingly complex and rapid pace of change in our world, lifelong learning has become essential not only for professionals but also for those they serve. Continuing professional education (CPE), an umbrella term used to describe the continuum of formal, nonformal, and informal learning opportunities that enable practicing professionals to continue to learn and to maintain professional competence across their careers, is the focus of this volume.

CPE emerged as a distinct area of focus within adult and continuing education in the 1960s, largely in the scholarly work of Houle (1980), who investigated postqualification professionals as they worked to keep up with new developments, gain mastery, understand the connection of their field to related disciplines, and grow as people as well as professionals. Houle observed professionals as agentic individuals capable of determining their learning needs and found that across professional groups, experiential knowledge acquired from practice was often seen as more useful than what was being acquired through formal continuing education. As a result, Houle cautioned against CPE approaches that merely increased formal educational offerings, emphasizing continuous and self-directed learning—a desire to continue to learn over the course of one's professional career—as the primary concern and focus for CPE. His classic text *Continuous Learning in the Professions* (1980) brought a decided learning focus to the debates on CPE, establishing a strong link between continuing education and lifelong learning. Houle's (1980) message to listen to the *experience* of professionals as a basis for supporting their professional learning has inspired educational scholars for the past 50 years.

Noting the lack of progress in the direction envisioned by Houle (1980), Mott and Daley (2000) offered a reformulated vision for CPE emphasizing that the "business" of CPE extended well beyond planning workshops to "the determination of how education can foster professional development programs that ultimately promote the ability to work in the uncertain, confusing, and dynamic world of professional practice for the betterment of clients" (p. 81). This collection is an update to the work of Daley and Mott and their many contributors, some who have contributed to this collection. The intent here, similarly, is to explore, analyze, question, and critique CPE trends and issues across a variety of contexts and to highlight new thinking and developments to assist providers and practitioners to reenvision their roles and to set new directions in the field of CPE.

Houle's (1980) ideas continue to inspire educational scholars today. This is evident in this collection, which advances earlier thinking about how professionals learn and develop knowledge from and during practice. Like Houle, the educational scholars who contributed to this collection continue to challenge the socially reproductive CPE that many professionals are engaged with, and to ask critical questions about the power relationships and interests of stakeholders. By inserting themselves into conversations about lifelong learning and researching spaces where knowledge production and practitioner training are being discussed and developed, they are shaping and reshaping understandings and practices of CPE.

In Chapter 1, Ronald M. Cervero and Barbara J. Daley, leading North American scholars in CPE, provide an historical account of issues and trends that have shaped the field and CPE practice. They contend that creating new systems of CPE is inherently a political process requiring negotiating and bargaining, not only among providers, but also within the social, professional, institutional, and educational agendas that frame the contested spaces within CPE.

Daley and Cervero (Chapter 2) update and expand previous work by Daley (2000) that explored how professionals learn and construct knowledge in the context of their practice by connecting concepts from their experiences and CPE activities. They advocate a learning-focused approach that acknowledges context and constructivist learning, and which takes account of expanded notions of transfer of learning and adoption of innovation.

Catherine A. Hansman (Chapter 3) adds to the conversation on learning, highlighting both formal and informal mentoring as influential in fostering interpersonal and interprofessional learning (i.e., collaborative, judgmental, reflective, and integrative capabilities), as well as the development of functions of leadership and management. Similar to other authors in this collection, Hansman exercises a critical gaze, highlighting unacknowledged and acknowledged power issues in mentoring relationships.

In Chapter 4, Patricia Cranton shifts the focus to CPE contexts, profiling CPE for teachers and university and college faculty members as usually formalized and instrumentally focused. She draws attention to the power inherent in disciplinary knowledge and teaching practice and encourages CPE that helps instructors to value communicative and emancipatory knowledge. Given the growth of online CPE offerings for instructors and faculty, she highlights teaching strategies that encourage greater authenticity and presence online and that employ democratic practices that can be modeled and practiced by the teachers and university and college faculty members in their practice settings.

Next, Laura L. Bierema (Chapter 5) profiles CPE in workplaces, where she finds highly interconnected and interdependent professionals struggle to keep pace with relentless change. She contends that there is global cynicism about CPE's effectiveness, relevance, and sustainability in the workplaces. In response, she offers an alternative conceptualization of professional learning and development as a basis for creating CPE that is responsive, relevant, and sustainable and that helps professionals in the workplace to more fluidly navigate the professional white water they encounter on a daily basis.

CPE in the health and medical professions is the focus of Chapter 6. Here, Elizabeth J. Tisdell and colleagues profile the emergence of a CPE program focused on teaching methodologies within a college of medicine. Coauthors and physician educators Margaret Wonjar and Elizabeth Sinz recount their experience as collaborators in the curriculum development process and their learning about adult education through the program that emerged. The authors offer a model depicting the processes of negotiating power and interest in the development of such a curriculum that they believe can be applied in other contexts.

In Chapter 7, Ashley Gleiman and Jeff Zacharakis highlight CPE in the military, and the continuum of CPE offerings made available at all levels of the military. They profile the shifting sands of support for CPE within this context and delve into critical debates revealing competing tensions embedded in military culture that challenge a unified vision for CPE across its systems.

In the final section, I synthesize the work of others in the collection, arriving at a "state of the field" update. CPE in the current moment, progress made post-Houle and future directions for research and practice are highlighted in this section.

Maureen Coady
Editor

References

Daley, B. J. (2000). Learning in professional practice. In V. W. Mott & Daley, B. J. (Eds.), *New Directions for Adult and Continuing Education: No. 86. Charting a course for continuing professional education* (pp. 33–43). San Francisco, CA: Jossey-Bass.

Houle, C. O. (1980). *Continuing learning in the professions*. San Francisco, CA: Jossey-Bass.

Mott, V. W., & Daley, B. J. (Eds.). (2000). *New Directions for Adult and Continuing Education: No. 86. Charting a course for continuing professional education*. San Francisco, CA: Jossey-Bass.

MAUREEN COADY is an associate professor and the chair of the Department of Adult Education at Saint Francis Xavier University, Antigonish, Nova Scotia, Canada.

This chapter analyzes the development and changes within continuing professional education and the influence of four contested spaces on this field of adult education practice.

Continuing Professional Education: A Contested Space

Ronald M. Cervero, Barbara J. Daley

Professional practice, whether it is housed in medicine, law, social work, nursing, or other professions, has always been characterized by a need to keep up to date so that individual professionals are bringing the best possible services to their clients. Professionals engage in a process of preprofessional education that often includes not only basic college courses but also a series of professional school courses, along with professional practice or clinical activities. Despite this in-depth level of preparation, most professionals realize that there will be a lifelong need to learn about new theories, research, evidence-based practice approaches, and advanced specialty knowledge. The continual development of professional practice and expertise is seen as one way to ensure quality in professional services provided to clients.

As such, continuing professional education (CPE) has existed since the early 1960s. CPE activities over the years have included courses, workshops, self-directed study, online activities, workplace inservice education, along with university-based offerings. Even with this large array of offerings designed to keep professionals current in their practice, CPE is still disputed, questioned, and challenged. As Cervero (1988) indicated, major questions in the field of CPE include (a) CPE for what purpose? (b) Who benefits from CPE? and (c) Who will provide CPE? CPE, at the present time, still exists in a contested space that is exemplified by the complexities of professional practice, educational delivery, and individual views.

This chapter examines the development and changes within CPE as a field of practice. Following a brief discussion of the history of CPE, the need for systems of CPE and the influence of four contested spaces (social, professional, institutional, and educational) within CPE are examined. This chapter concludes with a discussion of future trends.

New Directions for Adult and Continuing Education, no. 151, Fall 2016 © 2016 Wiley Periodicals, Inc.
Published online in Wiley Online Library (wileyonlinelibrary.com) • DOI: 10.1002/ace.20191

Background and Historical Perspectives

In the early 1900s, professional education, beginning with medical education, underwent a major transformation. Flexner (1910) analyzed medical schools across the United States and Canada, determining that approximately one third of medical schools produced poorly trained physicians. He recommended sweeping changes in the process of medical education that included the responsibility of all physicians "to generate new information and create progress in medical science, with assignment of this task to both laboratory and clinical scientists" (Duffy, 2011, p. 271). These recommendations led to the creation of carefully designed systems of medical education grounded in science, advancing research, and bringing a systematic, consistent level of preparation to medical school across the country. Additionally, these changes spurred states to develop licensure and certification processes for physicians and eventually other professions.

Since that time, most countries have engaged in the professionalization of their workforce. The Department for Professional Employees of the AFL-CIO (2015) estimated there are nearly 81 million professionals working in the United States. This amounts to 51% of the total workforce. These professionals provide healthcare services, educate children and adults, deliver rehabilitation services, supply legal support, and design the architectural infrastructure of our lives.

Following the Flexner report (1910), educational systems for preprofessional training were created, but systems for CPE lagged behind. Leaders in the professions assumed that professionals would keep up to date as part of their responsibilities of professional practice, and in the 1960s, most professions adopted some type of formal education programming for continuing education. The professions recognized that it was no longer possible to rely on only preprofessional education for a lifetime of practice. Early CPE programming was usually housed within each profession and was designed and offered by the profession itself. However, in the late 1960s, educators (Houle, 1980) began to recognize that many similarities existed in the processes of CPE. The content was different and related specifically to each profession, but the process of assessing learning needs, designing education offerings, teaching workshops, and evaluating programs was similar across various professions. These similarities led to the development of CPE as a field of practice.

During the 1970s, leaders in the professions and state licensing boards began to see a value in using CPE for relicensure and recertification (Cervero & Azzaretto, 1990). States developed relicensure programs that required professionals to complete a certain number of contact hours of CPE. By the 1980s, organized and comprehensive programs of CPE were developed across many professions (Cervero, 1988, 2011). Often these were operated by the same universities that prepared professionals in their preprofessional years. It was during this time that systems of accreditation for providers of CPE were developed. For example, the American Nurses Association developed an accreditation process whereby organizations could apply to have a single offering accredited or entire organization could be accredited as a provider of CPE (see http://www.nursecredentialing.org). These accreditation processes allowed the profession some control over the content of the offerings and the quality of delivery. However, the accreditation processes were at times cumbersome and added to the cost of program delivery. As a result, not all CPE providers were accredited.

In the 1990s, many CPE programs originally housed at universities were downsized. Employers of professionals started providing more and more educational offerings, including inservice education and new employee orientation along with CPE. Employers often felt it was more cost effective to provide education in house versus sending professionals outside of the organization for education. It was around this time that questions about the value of CPE for improving professional practice began to be raised across many professions, and CPE researchers were looking at both the outcome and impact of their work (Umble & Cervero, 1996).

In the 2000s, delivery systems of CPE have expanded to include more delivery and self-directed learning options (See Cranton in Chapter 4). These options provide flexibility for professionals to pick and choose the educational content and the time of study that is most convenient for them. For example, the University of Washington's website explains how continuing education programming has evolved in this decade to include interactive, web-based technologies, mobile devices, and social media (see: https://www.pce.uw.edu/why-choose-us). There has also been a push across the professions for evidence-based practice and educational programs that support this approach. Finally, more and more professions are moving toward an interdisciplinary approach in both preprofessional education and CPE.

Need for Systems of Continuing Professional Education

Despite these recent changes, however, the development of systems of CPE has not progressed as far as the development of systems of preprofessional education. CPE is only beginning to develop a more systematic approach to fostering professional education and learning for practice. Webster-Wright (2009, 2010) indicated that the provision of CPE has changed little because CPE providers tend to assume that knowledge is a commodity that is transferable to practice; that outcomes can be standardized and controlled, leading to a greater certainty in professional practice; and that professionals are deficient in areas of their practice and need to be "developed."

As such, the professions are currently in a transitional phase, attempting to determine the overall purpose, forms, locations, and delivery systems of CPE (Cervero, 2011; Cervero & Daley, 2010; Daley & Cervero, 2015). As an example of this transition, the Committee on Planning a Continuing Education Health Professions Institute conducted an in-depth examination of CPE that resulted in the Institute of Medicine (2010) report *Redesigning Continuing*

Education in the Health Professions. This report identified that "the absence of a comprehensive and well-integrated system of continuing education (CE) in the health professions is an important contributing factor to knowledge and performance deficiencies at the individual and system levels" (p. 1). This same report stated, "A new, comprehensive vision of professional development is needed to replace the culture that now envelops continuing education" (p. 3).

Contested Spaces of Continuing Professional Education

So the questions to be addressed in this transition are: What will these new systems of CPE look like? How will the needs of multiple stakeholders be met? Will interprofessional CPE become a reality and continue to expand across professions? As the field of CPE moves forward in developing new systems, the contested spaces of social, professional, institutional, and educational agendas need to be considered.

Social and Professional Agendas. In every profession, the knowledge available is used for multiple and sometimes conflicting purposes. Individuals within the professions have different values, beliefs, and approaches on how they should use their expertise. Because of this, different segments of each profession have different expectations on how they practice, how they use knowledge, and how new knowledge should be integrated into professional practice. These differences contribute to the social and professional agendas that are contested in creating systems of CPE. For example, Hirschkorn (2006) discussed the competing views between traditional medicine and complementary and alternative medicine (CAM), indicating that economic and political forces are at play in how practitioners provide care to clients. Moreover, "Biomedical providers seek to maintain their monopoly position in the provision of health services, and CAM providers, on the other hand, attempt to increase their status and share of the market" (Hirschkorn, 2006, p. 533).

It is not new nor is it surprising that these varying social and professional agendas exist. In trying to provide high-quality services to their clients, professionals will draw on not only their education and experience but also on multiple ideas vested in their belief systems. Professionals, as in the example cited previously, have to decide if they will offer CAM services to their clients. The professionals' role is to ask for whom and for what ends their expertise should be used (Cervero & Daley, 2010, 2011). As professionals' knowledge can serve conflicting social purposes, CPE, likewise, can and does serve many different purposes.

CPE is also being used to regulate and control professional practice. Most professions have some type of additional educational requirement that is needed for continuation of licensure. Different states monitor these requirements in varying fashions. Some use a random audit process to determine whether a sample group of professionals has met the requirements. Others require that the professional submit documentation of mandated CPE that has been completed during the relicensure process.

New Directions for Adult and Continuing Education • DOI: 10.1002/ace

Additionally, CPE is used as part of an advanced credentialing process. For example, the American Board of Internal Medicine, which is part of the American Board of Medical Specialties (ABMS), will certify doctors who meet specific educational, training and professional requirements (see http:// www.abim.org). After meeting the initial requirements and passing an examination in their specialty, physicians must enroll in a Maintenance of Certification (MOC) program. This MOC program requires that the physician earn 100 points over a 5-year period. Points must be earned in areas of medical knowledge, patient safety, practice assessment, and patient voice. Points can be earned in these areas in a variety of ways, including completing self-study modules, patient satisfaction surveys, chart audits, or quality improvement projects. The results of these endeavors are submitted to the American Board of Internal Medicine for the evaluation of the results and the awarding of points. What is interesting here is that certification renewal requires both development of knowledge and continual enhancement of medical practice. In this type of certification process, both education and practice development are included. As such, the CPE process is moving away from simply awarding contact hours for completing education programs to integrating education programs with a focus on maintaining competency for professional practice. The ABMS system gets away from what Queeney (2000) described as CPE that is too often "promoting the appearance of accountability but [doing] little or nothing to address the underlying issue of competence" (p. 378).

Institutional Agendas. The agendas of a variety of institutions also contribute to the contested space in CPE and need to be considered in the process of developing new systems of CPE. At the present time, CPE is provided to both individual practitioners and to organizations from a variety of sources. These sources may be individual consultants, universities, private companies, or professional organizations to name a few. However, the agendas of the various providers tend to center around four components: multiple goals, multiple providers, multiple modes of delivery, and collaboration among providers and professions (Cervero & Daley, 2010, 2011)

Multiple Goals. A wide variety of goals and purposes exist for the provision of CPE. These goals and purposes reflect the views of the individual and/or organization providing CPE. Goals may range from improving professional practice, to generating revenue, to elevating the status of the organization.

Some providers of CPE see it primarily as a revenue stream. These providers may sell CPE activities to the marketplace as their primary business. Organizations with this goal are mainly concerned with participation, customer satisfaction, and pricing of CPE activities. For example, private companies such as Nurse.com market online courses for nursing continuing education.

Within other organizations, the revenue from CPE offerings may be used to support and enhance the current business operations. CPE revenues are, at times, returned to the parent organization as a mechanism for providing funds to support their day-to-day operations. Usually when CPE is seen as contributing to a parent organization, the goals and vision of the parent organization are operationalized in the CPE program. These organizations are concerned about program feasibility and cost, but the primary goal is to support the parent organization.

A third group of organizations tend to see CPE as a mechanism for employee development. These organizations provide CPE as an employee benefit and retention strategy; they tend to be most concerned about making sure that employees have the skills needed to do their work and also that employees are committed to the organization because of the educational benefit provided.

Multiple Providers. Providers of CPE vary in size, scope, location, and level of service. In states where mandatory CPE exists, there tends to be a higher number of providers. Higher education has always been a provider of CPE and various arrangements exist for how CPE is organized in higher education. Some higher education providers have CPE based in professional schools so that it is linked with the faculty and preprofessional education. Here, the provider tends to focus on the content of the offerings and how those offerings contribute to the profession. Other higher education institutions have CPE centralized within an outreach or extension division where needs assessments, program planning, and marketing can be managed for a variety of professions.

Professional associations are also providers of CPE. Usually, CPE offered by professional associations will promote the goals and purposes of the association and, at times, may be a major revenue stream. Professional associations provide CPE to their members both as a mechanism for professional development and as a way for members to network and work toward meeting the association goals.

Additionally, for-profit businesses provide CPE. These organizations may provide only CPE, or they may be part of another business. Book companies, pharmaceutical companies, device manufacturing companies, and technology companies all provide CPE as part of their business strategy.

Finally, the workplace is a provider of CPE. Estimates indicate that the workplace may be the largest provider of CPE (Dass, 2014). Workplace CPE programs are most often designed for professionals employed at a specific organization. The content of these programs tends to be information that will assist professionals to function in their current or future job. For example, programs may include new employee orientation, training on new equipment, education on new computer systems, or discussion of changes in the way services are delivered to clients.

Multiple Modes of Delivery. Institutional agendas are also influenced by the variety in modes of delivery of CPE. Episodic, short-term delivery tends to be the predominant mode of CPE provision. This may include conferences that range from a single day to a week or short courses that are offered in a multi-week format. Face-to-face modes of delivery are popular in the provision of CPE because they offer both content and a way for professionals to talk with and share ideas with colleagues.

New Directions for Adult and Continuing Education • DOI: 10.1002/ace

More recently, CPE has taken advantage of the multiple modes of technology that can be used for delivery of educational program. This may include online courses, video conferencing, self-directed online study, podcasts, webinars, or online discussion groups.

Collaboration Among Providers and Professions. Finally, the level of collaboration among providers and professions will affect the institutional agenda and new systems of CPE that are created. Collaboration can help facilitate learning, increase the reach of CPE programs, and decrease the costs of CPE programs to consumers. And yet, some providers shy away from collaboration, seeing it as competition for the participation of learners instead.

Lately, there has been a strong move toward interprofessional education and to CPE as a mechanism to support and improve professional practice, particularly in the health professions. This type of collaboration involves providers from multiple professions working together to support the development of a team-based approach to professional practice and determining what each profession contributes to the client services offered. Based on this type of collaboration, interprofessional competencies can be established that guide the delivery of CPE.

In the United States, the Interprofessional Education Collaborative (American Association of Colleges of Nursing, Association of American Medical Colleges, American Dental Education Association, American Associations of Colleges of Pharmacy, Association of Schools of Public Health, and American Association of Colleges of Osteopathic Medicine) was established in 2009. (Schmitt Gilbert, Brandt & Weinstein 2013, p. 285)

This collaboration has defined interprofessional education as more than having learners from a variety of professions in the same educational offering. Rather, interprofessional education promotes an understanding of the functions of all health professions and how they each contribute in a team environment to promoting positive patient outcomes. Additionally, in this context, interactive adult education strategies are incorporated into all of the offerings.

Educational Agendas. Likewise, existing in the contested space of CPE are multiple educational agendas. As new systems of CPE are developed, the issues surrounding education, learning, performance, and evaluation will need to be addressed.

The contested space around the education agenda in CPE often centers on the question, CPE for what purpose (Cervero, 1988, 2000, 2001; Cervero & Daley, 2011)? A large part of what will drive the educational agenda in CPE is how providers view education and learning. Ito (2014), director of the MIT Media Lab, discussed in a recent TED talk how the Internet has fundamentally changed how people can work together, learn from each other, and network across countries. Joi Ito went on to state, "Education is what people do to you and learning is what you do to yourself" (10:03 min.). CPE providers may think this is an oversimplification of the relationship between learning and education, yet it points out a fundamental issue. If education is about developing programs, curricula, and competencies so that learners will take advantage of CPE, then how does that connect to and support the vast array of learning that individuals can engage in on their own? Do individual professionals need educational offerings created for them in this day and age, or can they access worldwide information that will support their own learning through the Internet? How will systems of CPE connect education and learning in an environment where access to information, knowledge, and new ideas is simply a Google™ search away? The quality of information, interactivity of technological offerings, and ability to discuss ideas with colleagues in this technologic world has the potential to surpass most of what can be created in traditional CPE.

The other issue affecting the various educational agendas in CPE is performance. Previously, professionals were expected to engage in CPE to demonstrate that they had acquired a certain number of contact hours, or seat time, in educational offerings. More recently, CPE is being developed and offered with the idea that it will improve a professional's performance and ultimately the services delivered to clients. For example, some organizations now expect professionals to incorporate an evidence-based approach into their own individual CPE efforts. In an evidence-based approach, professionals study the latest research in their professional area, decide how to implement that in their practice, make changes in their performance, and then document the results. This evidence-based approach could incorporate formal CPE, or it could be a completely self-directed process for the professional.

Finally, educational agendas in CPE are shaped by views on evaluation and effectiveness. The central question here is how effective CPE is in improving a professional's performance and ultimately client outcomes. As Webster-Wright (2009) indicated, "despite the fact that learning providers evaluate courses against stated learning outcomes, such learning may not be integrated into changes in every day work" (p. 704). She went on to note that this is most likely to occur when performance is emphasized over learning. And yet, multiple studies and systematic reviews have shown that continuing education can improve performance and client outcomes if following evidence-based principles, including focusing on outcomes considered important by learners and using multiple methods, multiple exposures, and active learning (Cervero & Gaines, 2015; Umble & Cervero, 1996).

Another major issue in understanding the effectiveness of CPE is related to understanding how evidence-based projects and self-directed learning through technology affect professional practice. If these types of learning endeavors are effective in maintaining and improving the quality of professional practice, then what is the role of CPE in the process? The other question here is whether individual professionals will engage actively and assume responsibility for this level of independence in managing their own learning. Webster-Wright (2010) suggested this question needs to be addressed in a way that respects and values the ability of professionals to direct their own learning.

Conclusion

Building systems of CPE is a much more complex process than creating preservice education programs for professionals that are limited to a specific length of time. CPE spans a professional's entire career, is offered by multiple providers, and is based on competing values and beliefs. It is evident that creating these new systems of CPE is a political process that will require bargaining and negotiation not only among providers but also within the social, professional, institutional, and educational agendas framing the contested spaces in CPE.

In the future, CPE will need to continue to adapt to adjustments in the various agendas that frame its social, political, and organizational context. CPE providers of the future will need to ensure that their programs are evidence based, interdisciplinary, technologically sophisticated, and linked to professional practice. High levels of collaboration between CPE educators and individuals practicing in the professions will be required to create the new systems needed with the ultimate goal of providing high quality professional services for the public good. As Wilson and Cervero (2014) indicated, "As the focus of continuing professional development is shifting away from time spent in educational activities to the demonstration of learning outcomes and competencies achieved, adult and continuing educators are well-positioned to provide leadership and expertise for this new direction" (p. 221).

References

AFL-CIO Department for Professional Employees. (2015). *The 0rofessional and technical workforce: DPE fact sheet.* Retrieved from http://dpeaflcio.org/programs-publications/issue-fact-sheets/the-professional-and-technical-workforce/.

Cervero, R. M. (1988). *Effective continuing education for professionals.* San Francisco, CA: Jossey-Bass.

Cervero, R. M., & Azzaretto, J. F. (1990). (Eds.). *Visions for the future of continuing professional education.* Athens, GA: The University of Georgia.

Cervero, R. M. (2000). Trends and issues in continuing professional education. In B. J. Daley & V. W. Mott (Eds.), *New Directions for Adult and Continuing Education: No. 86. Charting a course for continuing professional education* (pp. 3–12). San Francisco, CA: Jossey-Bass.

Cervero, R. M. (2001). Continuing professional education in transition, 1981–2000. *International Journal of Lifelong Learning, 20*(1–2), 16–30.

Cervero, R. M., & Daley, B. J. (2010). Continuing professional education: Multiple stakeholders and agendas. In P. Peterson, E. Baker, & B. McGaw (Eds.), *International encyclopedia of education* (Vol. 1, pp. 127–132). Oxford, UK: Elsevier.

Cervero, R. M. (2011). Lifespan professional development through practice-based education: Implications for the health professions. In G. J. Neimeyer & J. M. Taylor (Eds.), *Continuing professional development and lifelong learning: Issues, impacts, and outcomes* (pp. 265–276). New York, NY: Nova Science.

Cervero, R. M., & Daley, B. J. (2011). Continuing professional education: Multiple stakeholders and agendas. In K. Rubenson (Ed.), *Adult learning and education* (pp. 140–145). Oxford, UK: Elsevier.

Cervero, R. M., & Gaines, J. K. (2015). The impact of CME on physician performance and patient health outcomes: An updated synthesis of systematic reviews. *Journal of Continuing Education in the Health Professions, 35*(2), 131–137.

Daley, B. J., & Cervero, R. M. (2015). Continuing professional education, development and learning. In R. Poell, T. Rocco, & G. Roth (Eds.), *The Routledge companion to human resource development* (pp. 40–49). New York, NY: Routledge, Taylor and Francis Group.

Dass, B. (2014). *Adult and continuing professional education practices. CPE among professional providers*. Malaysia: Partridge Publishing.

Duffy, T. (2011). The Flexner Report—100 years later. *Yale Journal of Biology and Medicine, 84*(3), 269–276.

Flexner, A. (1910). *Medical education in the United States and Canada: A report to the Carnegie Foundation for the Advancement of Teaching*. New York, NY: Carnegie Foundation.

Hirschkorn, K. A. (2006). Exclusive versus everyday forms of professional knowledge: Legitimacy claims in conventional and alternative medicine. *Sociology of Health & Illness, 28*, 533–557. doi:10.1111/j.1467-9566.2006.00506.x

Houle, C. O. (1980). *Continuing learning in the professions*. San Francisco, CA: Jossey-Bass.

Institute of Medicine Committee on Planning a Continuing Health Professional Education Institute. (2010). *Redesigning continuing education in the health professions*. Washington, DC: National Academies Press. Retrieved from http://www.nap.edu/catalog.php?record_id=12704.

Ito, J. (2014, March). *Want to innovate? Become a now-ist* [Video]. Retrieved from http://www.ted.com/talks/joi_ito_want_to_innovate_become_a_now_ist?language=en.

Queeney, D. S. (2000). Continuing professional education. In A. Wilson & E. Hayes (Eds.), *Handbook of adult and continuing education* (pp. 375–391). San Francisco, CA: Jossey-Bass.

Schmitt, M., Gilbert, J., Brandt, B., & Weinstein, R. (2013). The coming of age for interprofessional education and practice. *American Journal of Medicine, 126*(4), 284–288.

Umble, K., & Cervero, R. (1996). Impact studies in continuing education for health professionals: Critique of the research syntheses. *Evaluation and the Health Professions, 19*(2), 148–174.

Webster-Wright, A. (2009). Reframing professional development through understanding authentic professional learning. *Review of Educational Research, 79*(2), 702–739. doi:10.3102/0034654308330970

Webster-Wright, A. (2010). *Authentic professional learning: Making a difference through learning at work (Professional and Practice Based Learning Series)*. London, UK: Springer.

Wilson, A., & Cervero, R. (2014). Continuing professional education in the United States: A strategic analysis of current and future directions. In B. Käpplinger & S. Robak (Eds), *Changing configurations of adult education in transitional times: International perspectives in different countries* (pp. 211–222). New York, NY: Peter Lang.

RONALD M. CERVERO *is professor in the Department of Lifelong Education, Administration, and Policy and Associate Vice President for Instruction at the University of Georgia.*

BARBARA J. DALEY *is professor of Adult and Continuing Education in the Department of Administrative Leadership at the University of Wisconsin–Milwaukee.*

2

This chapter is an update and expansion of previous work and explores how professionals construct knowledge in the context of their practice by connecting concepts from their experiences and continuing professional education activities.

Learning as the Basis for Continuing Professional Education

Barbara J. Daley, Ronald M. Cervero

Learning within continuing professional education (CPE) programs is a central issue for professional practice development. As providers of CPE, we often make the assumption that attendance at CPE programs constitutes learning for professionals and that they will automatically use this information once they return to their work sites.

But what do we, as CPE providers, really know about how participants learn to use new information? We know that many professionals attend CPE only to shelve the large handouts and course materials they receive, never to look at them again (Nowlen, 1988; Webster-Wright, 2009). We know that the theory or new knowledge taught in CPE programs is seldom transferred immediately and directly to the practice arena (Foley & Kaiser, 2013). We know that most CPE programs are more effective in teaching novices than they are in fostering the professional development of experts (Daley, 1999; Reich, Rooney, & Boud, 2015). And, finally, we know there are factors in the work environment that inhibit practitioners from incorporating what they have learned in a CPE program into their practice (Daley, 1997, 2001; Eraut, 1994, 2007; Webster-Wright, 2010).

Despite the issues identified in the preceding paragraph, we also know that practitioners do use information from CPE programs in their practice—often in ways that are totally unintended by program planners (Daley, 2001). We know that it is extremely difficult to evaluate the outcomes of CPE programs because use of the program's material is often idiosyncratic to the learner (Ottoson, 2000).

To be truly effective in CPE, we must include a model of learning (Cervero, 1988) at the heart of our education practice. As Eraut (1994) explained, behind "professional education lies a remarkable ignorance about professional learning" (p. 40). Our previous models of learning have relied

NEW DIRECTIONS FOR ADULT AND CONTINUING EDUCATION, no. 151, Fall 2016 © 2016 Wiley Periodicals, Inc.
Published online in Wiley Online Library (wileyonlinelibrary.com) • DOI: 10.1002/ace.20192

on the ideas of technical rationality (Houle, 1980), transfer of learning, and adoption of innovation (Boud & Hager, 2011). In these views, knowledge for professional practice was created in one location, often a university setting, disseminated through CPE programs, and then transferred to or adopted in professional practice. Using these models of learning, educators tended to create educational programs that provided up-to-date information rather than fostering a continuum of professional practice development (See Cervero & Daley, Chapter 1).

In this chapter, we advocate reframing CPE to include a constructivist view of learning created by linking professional practice, context, and knowledge into an integrated learning system. This chapter expands the notions of transfer of learning and adoption of innovation, proposing a perspective of learning from which CPE can be reframed. We have chosen to provide here an expansion and update of previous work (Daley, 2000). We have added new literature, updated examples, and highlighted changes in professional practice. The basic premise, however, remains the same: learning is the basis of CPE.

Previous Learning Model in Continuing Professional Education

Cervero (1988) proposed a model for learning in the professions based on an understanding of how professionals "develop knowledge through practice" (p. 39). He incorporated cognitive psychology, reflective practice (Schön, 1987), and studies of expertise (Benner, 1984; Dreyfus & Dreyfus, 1985) into this model. Cervero (1988) advocated that CPE providers develop a critical model of the learner that integrates the development of two forms of knowledge: technical knowledge and practical knowledge, or as Schön (1987) described, knowing *that* and knowing *how*. Both forms of knowledge were necessary to incorporate scientific principles with cases, examples, and real life experiences. Cervero's (1988) model was instrumental in linking learning theory with professional practice.

Expanded Model of Learning in Continuing Professional Education

Recent research (Daley, 2001; Webster-Wright, 2009) indicates that professionals construct a knowledge base for themselves in the context of their practice by linking concepts from new knowledge with their practice experiences. At this point, they actively make decisions on how to incorporate new knowledge into the context of practice based on their interpretations of the environment. In a previous study interviewing professionals about how they learned, Daley (2001) asked a nurse how she made connections between the client care she provided and knowledge from CPE programs. The nurse responded:

> Well, I don't think of it like that, I mean I can't really say what helps me deal with what. I think of it more like creating mosaics. I mean, you have all these

little pieces that come from all over and in and of themselves they don't mean much, but when you put them together you have a beautiful picture. Continuing education and client care are more like that for me. I take little pieces of what I learn from many places and put them together until I have my own picture. (Daley, 2001, p. 47)

This metaphor of *creating a mosaic* depicts the process of actively constructing a knowledge base from practice.

In expanding Cervero's (1988) model of learning, we need to further develop an understanding of how knowledge is constructed, how it is linked with professional practice, and how the context affects the process (see Figure 2.1). Additionally, in newer work, Dirkx, Gilley, and Maycunich-Gilley (2004) indicated that the identity of the professional is intimately intertwined with the process of developing and sustaining knowledge for professional practice.

Figure 2.1. Model of Learning in CPE (reprinted with permission Copyright © 2000 John Wiley & Sons)

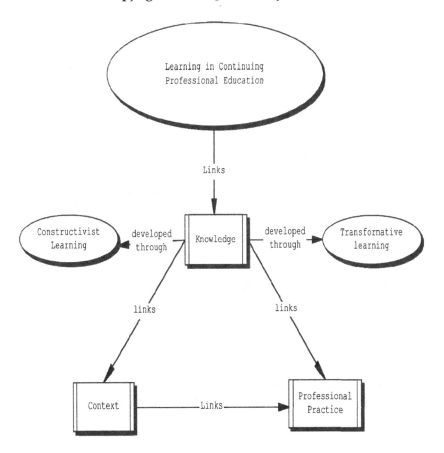

Knowledge Construction for Professional Practice. In the model of learning depicted in Figure 2.1, knowledge is viewed as a social construction of information that occurs through a process of constructivist and transformative learning.

Combining a constructivist and transformative perspective allows us to understand how the learner creates a knowledge base yet changes that knowledge base when faced with practice experiences. Context and professional practice are then linked to knowledge development to complete the learning model depicted.

Constructivist Learning Theory. Constructivists believe that individuals create knowledge by linking new information with past experiences (Jonassen & Land, 2012; Novak, 1998). Within a constructivist framework, the learner progressively differentiates concepts into more and more complex understandings and also reconciles abstract understanding with concepts garnered from previous experience. Learners make knowledge meaningful by the ways in which they establish connections among knowledge learned, previous experiences, and the context in which they find themselves.

In summary, constructivists believe that learning is a process of probing deeply the meaning of experiences in our lives and developing an understanding of how these experiences shape understanding. Within a constructivist framework, learning activities are designed to foster an integration of thinking, feeling, and acting while helping participants learn how to learn (Jonassen & Land, 2012; Novak & Gowin, 1984). In recent work, Coady (2015) took this idea one step further when she summarized Dirkx et al.'s (2004) view that the self is an active part of the coconstruction of knowledge and lifelong learning in professional practice. As Coady indicated, a major aim in CPE and development should include promoting self-understanding.

Learning in the context of professional practice is also informed by the growing body of work in the area of situated cognition (Paige & Daley, 2009). Situated cognition can be conceptualized as having four interrelated learning aspects: (a) learning that is situated in the context of authentic practice, (b) transfer limited to similar situations, (c) learning as a social phenomenon, and (d) learning that relies on use of prior knowledge. According to Boud and Hagar (2011):

> Learning is a normal part of working. It occurs through practice in work settings from addressing the challenge and problems that arise. Most learning takes place not through formalized activities but through the exigencies of practice with peers and others, drawing on expertise that is accessed in response to need. (p. 22)

They concluded that "problem solving in which professionals tackle challenges which progressively extend their existing capabilities and learn with and from each other appears to be a frequent form of naturalistic development" (p. 22).

New Directions for Adult and Continuing Education • DOI: 10.1002/ace

Finally, learning in professional practice is informed by an evolving understanding of the self (Dirkx et al., 2004). This growing and developing understanding of the self is also situated in the context of professional practice. As Dirkx et al. stated, "New approaches to professional development suggest practitioners' lifelong learning in professional practice is characterized by an evolving critical awareness of the self in relationship with itself, with others, and with its social and cultural context" (p. 41).

Transformative Learning. Constructivist learning theory, situated cognition, and an understanding of the self help us understand how professionals acquire knowledge, how they make use of their experiences, and how they learn through their practice. In our experience, there is another level of learning that goes beyond what we can understand from constructivist frameworks. Professionals will often describe how they learned topics in formal education programs only to have their ideas on those topics changed in the context of practice. An emotional encounter with a client or a disorienting dilemma (Baumgartner, 2012; Mezirow, 2009) in practice may be as important in transforming professionals' perspectives as knowledge acquired in CPE courses. Transformative learning adds to our understanding of these changes.

Transformative learning (Mezirow, 1991, 1997aa, 1997b, 2009) expands our understanding of constructing knowledge by defining learning as a critically reflective process wherein the learner ultimately assesses previous understandings to determine whether those assumptions still hold in the learner's present situation. Adults learn within this framework by adding to or transforming old meaning schemes, acquiring new meaning schemes, or transforming perspectives.

An expanded model of learning in professional practice needs to link the theoretical perspectives of transformative and constructivist learning. Linking these two perspectives provides an explanation of how professionals initially acquire information and then change their understanding of that information based on experience. For example, a social worker described how her understanding of resistance in working with involuntary clients changed her views on the connections between social work and politics. She indicated that her basic education "labeled people as resistant" (Daley, 2001, p. 48), explaining the impact of her practice on this perspective:

> When somebody comes to you with a problem, I learned that you don't have to spend as much time fixing that person as you do fixing the things around them in the environment. If you listen, you know it is not so much resistance; but it is racism, it is poverty. I learned to reconceptualize resistance and focus not so much on the individual in a therapeutic sense, but to focus on the system, and to be an advocate at the system level. (p. 48)

This social worker indicated that she had constructed a new meaning of the concept of resistance through her practice and that she had transformed her perspective so that her interventions with clients were on a much broader level.

In another example, a lawyer shared how his understanding of professional practice was transformed. He stated:

> When I first started practicing, I would become very aggressive in divorce cases about dividing up assets. That was what I learned; I made sure that I evaluated assets to maximize my client's side of the ledger, and I made sure they were divided in such a way that my client would get absolute top dollar and I would fight very forcefully and aggressively. When I look at things now, I think it is important that people get the dollar amount that they should, but I think there are other aspects that come into play also, like a continuing good relationship between the husband and wife, if it is possible to preserve that—such as continuing good relationships with the children, such as peace of mind, such as not spending a great deal of money on attorney fees, such as avoiding a trial and the bad relationship that can carry over for years between parties. (Daley, 2001, pp. 48–49)

These examples highlight how professionals engage in subjective reframing that fosters learning from their experiences and transforms their practice. Recently, Servage (2008) has expanded the integration of transformative learning and professional practice by advocating for the use of transformative learning theory as the guiding framework for collaborative practices within professional learning communities.

Linking Knowledge and Context. In the expanded model of learning presented in Figure 2.1, *context* refers to the place where professionals provide care or deliver services to clients. The relationship of context to practice is particularly important because, in today's environment, professionals are considered organizational employees rather than free, autonomous decision-makers (Wilson & Cervero, 2014). Fenwick (2012) and others (Reich et al., 2015) pointed out that these changing conditions necessitate a deeper understanding of organizational professions, the impact of bureaucracy on them, and changing organizational dynamics on professional work.

In the model of learning presented here, Bolman and Deal's (2013) framework is added as a way to clarify the connections between knowledge and context. Their model delineates that organizations can be viewed through four different frames: structural, human resources, political, and symbolic. The *structural frame* uses sociology concepts and emphasizes formal roles, defined relationships, and structures that fit the organizational environment and technology. The *human resources frame*, posits that organizations have individuals with needs and feelings that must be taken into account so that individuals can learn, grow, and change. The *political frame* analyzes conflict as part of organizational processes. Within this view, the organization is composed of separate groups competing for power and resources. The *symbolic frame* sees organizations as tribes with cultures propelled by rituals, ceremonies, stories, heroes, and myths (Bolman & Deal, 2013). By viewing a model of learning through these imaginary frames, CPE providers can begin to understand the impact context has on knowledge construction.

In professional practice, the context shapes how professionals look at new information, influencing not only what information professionals seek to learn but also what information they try to incorporate into their professional practice. In studies with professionals, Daley (2001) found that Bolman and Deal's (2013) organizational frames affect the knowledge use of nurses, social workers, and lawyers in ways unique to each profession. For instance, nurses would use the political frame to construct knowledge differently than lawyers or social workers would. Nurses literally screened out information from their practice based on the perception of the political frame. When asked about how organizational politics influence their use of knowledge, one nurse said, "Well, if I don't have the power to use the information I just don't even share it." However, a social worker responding to the same question explained, "Well, just because the door is closed, does not mean it is locked. There is always a way around that." Social workers indicated that they viewed dealing with the political context as an integral part of their advocacy role. Lawyers, on the other hand, seemed to view their work as one on one with a client. If they chose to use new information in their practice they did so, regardless of the political system. The important point here is that the context affects each of these professions in a manner that is unique to that profession, thus offering the CPE provider important information for program planning and evaluation.

Developing Professional Practice. Within the CPE literature, two schools of thought exist as to how professionals develop within their practice arenas. One perspective describes professional development as simply the enhancement of thought and information processing skills; the second views professional development as the enhancement of expertise through an artistic-intuitive approach. Both of these views are included in the model of learning described in Figure 2.1.

In the first view, professional development is described as a rational process of information processing, problem solving, decision making, and clinical reasoning and judgment (Ericsson, Charness, Feltovich, & Hoffman, 2006; Fonteyn, 1991). Results from studies involving lawyers (Daley, 2001), for instance, have indicated that as their practice developed, they learned to sort through extraneous issues and get to the heart of the matter quickly and efficiently. They claimed they seldom used an intuitive thought process, but rather used a highly analytical one that narrows and reduces information to its most elemental form. For instance, one lawyer stated, "The main thing I have to do in my practice, is sort through all the information the client presents and get to the bottom line issue to analyze how the issue fits with the law."

Alternatively, the literature presents a second view of professional development that is described as attaining expertise by taking a more intuitive approach to the topic (Benner, 1984; Dreyfus & Dreyfus, 1985; Ericsson et al., 2006; Eraut, 1994; Schön, 1987). This view of professional development encompasses the ideas of artistry, reflection, and alternative ways of knowing in professional development. Benner's classic study (1984) expands our understanding of the development of professional practice by identifying domains of practice on a continuum from novice to expert. This continuum, based on the Dreyfus Model of Skill Acquisition (Dreyfus & Dreyfus, 1985), suggests that professionals develop from novice to expert as they learn to rely on past concrete experiences rather than on abstract principles, as they understand situations as integrated wholes rather than as discrete parts, and as they begin to act as involved performers rather than detached observers (Benner, 1984). Newer work (see Kinsella & Pittman, 2012) supports this perspective and indicates that phronesis, or practical wisdom, is essential in professional development.

One of the most interesting findings in studies comparing novice and expert nurses (Daley, 1999) was that experts have developed an understanding of their own learning processes. Expert nurses, for instance, have learned how to learn in the context of their practice. They know how to search out information and make connections between the new information and their experience. Furthermore, they are willing to change their practice based on the new knowledge they create. Novice nurses, on the other hand, tend to use learning strategies that are more contingent on others and on the written rules.

In the preceding sections of this chapter, a model for understanding the learning in CPE (see Figure 2.1) was proposed based on combining literature, research, and experience in the areas of constructivist learning, transformative learning, organizational context, information processing, and professional practice development. This model offers a way by which CPE providers can integrate learning, professional development, and context within their educational activities.

Implications for the Provision of Continuing Professional Education: Creating Systems of Learning

The model of learning for CPE described in this chapter has a number of implications for CPE practice. Obviously, this is not an all-inclusive model of learning, and it is embedded in assumptions about the nature of knowledge in professional practice and the contexts of knowledge use.

Enhancing professional practice development requires a model of learning that incorporates the professional along with identify (Dirkx et al., 2004), the work environment, and the practice itself into our educational endeavors. Yet, basing our CPE practice on a model of learning or a learning system is a change in mindset for the majority of CPE providers, because this shifts the role from developer of specific program content to facilitator of learning, growth, and change in professional practice. It means that when CPE providers create programs, they will need to actively plan and incorporate methods that encourage participants to link the content of the program to their actual practice and their work environments.

But how can this be accomplished? There are already many educational tools that foster both a constructivist and transformative view of learning.

New Directions for Adult and Continuing Education • DOI: 10.1002/ace

Consider such tools as concept maps (Daley, 2010), reflective journals (Brookfield, 1995), Venn diagrams (Novak, 1998), analysis of practice exemplars (Benner, 1984), critical incidents (Brookfield, 1995), action learning (Brooks & Watkins, 1994), and creating professional learning communities (deGroot, Endedijk, Jaarsma, Simons, & van Beukelen, 2014; Eraut, 1994; Servage, 2008). All can be used to foster a constructivist, transformative, context-based professional practice development program. What these tools have in common is that they create a record of professional practice events or experiences and then allow the professional to reflect upon them and make connections between them and the context of their practice.

Additionally, since the model in Figure 2.1 was originally proposed (see Daley, 2000), many professions have begun engaging in interprofessional education and evidence-based practice (see Cervero & Daley, Chapter 1). Both evidence-based practice and interprofessional education have the potential to enhance professional practice development. CPE providers can use an evidence-based practice approach to create offerings that have professionals decide how to incorporate the latest research results into their practice and then evaluate the changes they see. Linking an evidence-based practice approach with action learning is an example of how CPE providers can ground their work in a learning model. Additionally, to incorporate an interdisciplinary perspective in their work, CPE providers can create offerings that explore practice-based cases from the perspective of multiple professions.

The key is to change our mindset as CPE providers and to open our program planning and evaluation to new ideas and different ways to incorporate a view of the learner and learning into our CPE practice. Our main challenge as CPE providers is to understand that transfer of learning and adoption of innovation are part of the knowledge construction process and an integral part of professional learning. Thus, when we view professional learning as constructivist and transformative, when we link both context and professional practice to the learning, we have then situated and integrated a holistic, rather than a segmented and partitioned, view of knowledge development.

Note

This chapter is a revision and update of previous work. Significant portions of this work were published as Daley, B. (2000). Learning in professional practice. In V. Mott & B. Daley (Eds.), *New Directions for Adult and Continuing Education: No. 86. Charting a course for continuing professional education: Reframing professional practice* (pp. 33–42). San Francisco, CA: Jossey-Bass. *[Update and revision of this work with permission of Wiley Global Permissions,* © *2000 John Wiley & Sons.]*

References

Baumgartner, L. (2012). Mezirow's theory of transformative learning from 1975 to present. In E. Taylor, P. Cranton, & Associates (Eds.), *The handbook of transformative learning theory, research and practice* (pp. 99–115). San Francisco, CA: Jossey-Bass.

Benner, P. (1984). *From novice to expert: Excellence and power in clinical nursing practice.* Menlo Park, CA: Addison-Wesley.

Bolman, L., & Deal, T. (2013). *Reframing organizations: Artistry, choice and leadership* (5th ed.). San Francisco, CA: Jossey-Bass.

Boud, D., & Hager, P. (2011). Rethinking continuing professional development through changing metaphors and locations in professional practice. *Studies in Continuing Education, 34*(1), 17–30. doi:10.1080/0158037X.2011.608656

Brookfield, S. (1995). *Becoming a critically reflective teacher.* San Francisco, CA: Jossey-Bass.

Brooks, A., & Watkins, K. (Eds.). (1994). *New Directions for Adult and Continuing Education: No. 63. The emerging power of action inquiry technologies.* San Francisco, CA: Jossey-Bass.

Cervero, R. (1988). *Effective continuing education for professionals.* San Francisco, CA: Jossey-Bass.

Coady, M. (2015). From Houle to Dirkx: Continuing professional education (CPE). A critical "state of the field" review. *Canadian Journal for Studies in Adult Education, 27*(3), 27–40.

Daley, B. (1999). Novice to expert: An exploration of how professionals learn. *Adult Education Quarterly, 49*(4), 133–147.

Daley, B. (1997). Creating mosaics: The interrelationships of knowledge and context. *Journal of Continuing Education in Nursing, 28*(3), 102–114.

Daley, B. (2000). Learning in professional practice. In V. Mott & B. Daley (Eds.), *New Directions for Adult and Continuing Education: No. 86. Charting a course for continuing professional education: Reframing professional practice* (pp. 33–42). San Francisco, CA: Jossey-Bass.

Daley, B. (2001). Learning and professional practice: A study of four professions. *Adult Education Quarterly, 52*(1), 39–54.

Daley, B. (2010). Concept maps: Practice applications in adult education and human resource development [Perspectives on Practice]. *New Horizons in Adult Education and Human Resource Development, 24*(2). Retrieved from http://education.fiu.edu/newhorizons

deGroot, E., Endedijk, M., Jaarsma, D. C., Simons, P. R.-J., & van Beukelen, P. (2014). Critically reflective dialogues in learning communities of professionals. *Studies in Continuing Education, 36*(1), 15–37. doi:10.1080/0158037X.2013.779240

Dirkx, J., Gilley, J. W., & Maycunich-Gilley, A. (2004). Change theory in CPE and HRD: Toward a holistic view of learning and change in work. *Advances in Developing Human Resources, 6*(1), 35–51. doi:10.1177/1523422303260825

Dreyfus, H., & Dreyfus, S. (1985). *Mind over machine: The power of human intuition and expertise in the era of the computer.* New York, NY: Free Press.

Ericsson, K., Charness, N., Feltovich, P., & Hoffman, R. (Eds.). (2006). *The Cambridge handbook of expertise and expert performance.* New York, NY: Cambridge University Press.

Eraut, M. (1994). *Developing professional knowledge and competence.* Washington, DC: Falmer Press.

Eraut, M. (2007). Learning from other people in the workplace. *Oxford Review of Education, 33*(4), 403–422. doi:10.1080/03054980701425706

Fenwick, T. (2012). Understanding transitions in professional practice and learning: Towards new questions for research. *Journal of Workplace Learning, 25*(6), 352–367.

Foley, J., & Kaiser, L. (2013). Learning transfer and its intentionality in adult and continuing education. In L. Kaiser, K. Kaminski, & J. Foley (Eds.), *New Directions for Adult and Continuing Education: No. 137. Learning transfer in adult education* (pp. 5–15). San Francisco, CA: Jossey-Bass.

Fonteyn, M. (1991). Research review and implications for practice: Implications of clinical reasoning studies for critical care nursing. *Focus on Critical Care, 18*(4), 322–327.

Houle, C. O. (1980). *Continuing learning in the professions.* San Francisco, CA: Jossey-Bass.

Jonassen, D., & Land, S. (Eds.). (2012). *Theoretical foundations of learning environments* (2nd ed.). New York, NY: Routledge Taylor and Francis Group.

Kinsella, E., & Pitman, A. (Eds.). (2012). *Phronesis as professional knowledge: Practice wisdom in the professions.* Rotterdam, The Netherlands: Sense Publishers.

Mezirow, J. (1991). *Transformative dimensions of adult learning*. San Francisco, CA: Jossey-Bass.

Mezirow, J. (1997a). Transformation theory out of context. *Adult Education Quarterly, 48*(1), 60–62.

Mezirow, J. (1997b). Transformative learning: Theory to practice. In P. Cranton (Ed.), *New Directions for Adult and Continuing Education: No. 74. Transformative learning in action: Insights from practice* (pp. 5–12). San Francisco, CA: Jossey-Bass.

Mezirow, J. (2009). Transformative learning theory. In J. Mezirow, E. Taylor, & Associates (Eds.), *Transformative learning in practice: Insights from community, workplace and higher education* (pp. 18–31). San Francisco, CA: Jossey-Bass.

Nowlen, P. (1988). *A new approach to continuing education for business and the professions: The performance model*. New York, NY: Macmillan.

Novak, J. (1998). *Learning, creating and using knowledge: Concept Maps*™ *as facilitative tools in schools and corporations*. Mahwah, NJ: Lawrence Erlbaum Associates.

Novak, J., & Gowin, B. (1984). *Learning how to learn*. Cambridge, MA: Cambridge University Press.

Ottoson, J. (2000). Evaluation of continuing professional education: Toward a theory of our own. In V. Mott & B. Daley (Eds.), *New Directions for Adult and Continuing Education: No. 86. Charting a course for continuing professional education: Reframing professional practice* (pp. 43–53). San Francisco, CA: Jossey-Bass.

Paige, J. B., & Daley, B. J. (2009). Situated cognition: A learning framework to support and guide high-fidelity simulation. *Clinical Simulation in Nursing, 5*(3), e97–e103. doi:10.1016/j.ecns.2009.03.120

Reich, A., Rooney, D., & Boud, D. (2015). Dilemmas in continuing professional learning: Learning inscribed in frameworks or elicited from practice. *Studies in Continuing Education, 37*(2), 131–141. doi:10.1080/0158037X.2015.1022717

Schön, D. A. (1987). *Educating the reflective practitioner: Toward a new design for teaching and learning in the professions*. San Francisco, CA: Jossey-Bass.

Servage, L. (2008). Critical and transformative practices in professional learning communities. *Teacher Education Quarterly, 35*(1), 63–77.

Webster-Wright, A. (2009). Reframing professional development through understanding authentic professional learning. *Review of Educational Research, 79*(2), 702–739. doi:10.3102/0034654308330970

Webster-Wright, A. (2010). *Authentic professional learning: Making a difference through learning at work (Professional and Practice Based Learning Series)*. London, UK: Springer.

Wilson, A., & Cervero, R. (2014). Continuing professional education in the United States: A strategic analysis of current and future directions. In B. Käpplinger & S. Robak (Eds.), *Changing configurations in adult education in transitional times: International perspectives in different countries* (pp. 211–222). New York, NY: Peter Lang.

BARBARA J. DALEY *is professor of Adult and Continuing Education in the Department of Administrative Leadership at the University of Wisconsin–Milwaukee.*

RONALD M. CERVERO *is professor in the Department of Lifelong Education, Administration, and Policy and associate vice president for Instruction at the University of Georgia.*

3

This chapter examines the role of mentoring in continuing professional education from a critical perspective, addressing informal and formal mentoring relationships while highlighting their potential to encourage critical reflection, learning, and coconstruction of knowledge.

Mentoring and Informal Learning as Continuing Professional Education

Catherine A. Hansman

In a recent broadcast of *The Late Show with Stephen Colbert* (Katsir & Moreschi, 2015), American actor Kevin Spacey discussed his work mentoring younger professional actors, mentioning that he himself had been mentored by the actor Jack Lemmon. Spacey explained that Lemmon's philosophy for mentoring others was "if you are doing well in the business, you help others starting up and send the elevator back down to bring them up—it's your obligation." Although *Late Show* host Colbert responded that it was a wonderful image to send the elevator back down for the young people, he quizzically asked "But they're young; can't they take the steps?" However humorous Colbert's question was meant to be, it illustrates the potential power of mentoring relationships in continuing professional education (CPE). Organizations or professional associations may make decisions regarding who may have opportunities in supportive mentoring relationships—taking the elevator—or who may not be provided mentoring opportunities for professional development and must take the stairs in a slower and more onerous route for learning.

Queeney defined CPE as "the education of professional practitioners, regardless of their practice setting, that follows their preparatory curriculum and extends their learning … throughout their careers" (as cited in Queeney, 2000, p. 375). She further contended that CPE should "go beyond simply providing information and teaching technical procedures; it must help professionals build their collaborative, judgmental, reflective and integrative capabilities" (p. 379). However, as Cervero and Daley discussed in Chapter 1, the enduring challenge is to create systems of learning that will foster improvement of professional practice.

Perhaps one CPE approach to address organizational and individual growth and development within professional practice is through formal and informal mentoring relationships. However, mentoring others in professional

New Directions for Adult and Continuing Education, no. 151, Fall 2016 © 2016 Wiley Periodicals, Inc.
Published online in Wiley Online Library (wileyonlinelibrary.com) • DOI: 10.1002/ace.20193

settings or planning formal mentoring programs for professional development can be complicated. Issues may arise, including the availability or lack of mentors. As well, organizational or other types of power structures may impede informal learning and mentoring relationships. Nevertheless, supportive mentoring relationships may provide context-rich learning opportunities for mentees and their mentors in CPE programs and in workplaces that support professional development. Mullen (2012) claimed "the spectrum of traditional and alternative theories of mentoring is influential in the interpersonal areas of learning, socialization, and professional development, as well as the organizational functions of leadership, management, and preparation" (p. 10). However, in many cases mentoring relationships, especially nonformalized ones, and informal learning are often undervalued in the context of CPE, possibly because they are invisible and difficult to analyze for effectiveness. Indeed, as de Laat and Schreurs (2013) explained, "more spontaneous and informal ways of learning are largely overlooked in organizations, and thus the effects of informal learning remain invisible" (p. 1422).

Learning in CPE should be located in day-to-day work. Mentoring relationships, therefore, either in formal or informal contexts, may provide a vehicle for fostering professional learning. This chapter examines the role of mentoring in CPE from a critical perspective, addressing informal and formal mentoring relationships while highlighting their potential to encourage critical reflection, learning, and coconstruction of knowledge.

Formal and Informal Learning

Houle (1980) defines learning as "the process by which people gain knowledge, sensitiveness, or mastery of skills through experience or study" (p. xi). Formal and informal learning appear to exist in two distinct paradigms, with formal learning viewed as "acquisitional and individual ... vertical or propositional knowledge within education institutions" (Malcolm, Hodkinson, & Colley, 2003, p. 314). Formal learning may take place in institutions or professional organizations and lead to certificates, diplomas, or other credentials for learners. Eraut (2004, 2007) discussed learning as occurring on a continuum, with formal learning on one end of the scale and informal learning on the other.

Informal learning is frequently regarded as "the natural accompaniment to everyday life" (Colley, Hodkinson, & Malcolm, 2003, p. 8), in that people participate in learning activities through their everyday undertakings and may not even be cognizant of their learning. Cervero (1992) promoted the idea of real-world learning embedded in CPE programs and models, asserting that "popular wisdom among practicing professionals is that the knowledge they acquire from practice [informal learning] is far more useful than what they acquire from formal forms of education" (p. 91). Further, Sandlin, Wright, and Clark (2011) contended that informal learning spaces and public pedagogies inform learning and identity development outside of formal learning

New Directions for Adult and Continuing Education • DOI: 10.1002/ace

contexts. However, Malcolm et al. (2003) suggested that informal learning occurs within formal learning, perhaps on a continuum, and that the value of isolating informal from formal learning is to draw attention to its constituent nature.

Informal learning is considered more spontaneous and may consist of ad hoc or spur-of-the-moment learning activities. de Laat and Schreurs (2013) stressed that:

> The effects of informal learning remain invisible. Yet there is a large body of literature that convincingly shows that these forms of spontaneous work related learning are important drivers for ongoing professional development, and that such learning does not occur in isolation. (p. 1422)

Learning in CPE is deeply connected to the work people do with others in collaborative pairs or groups, fostered through the formal and informal social networks and communities formed by professionals, such as mentoring relationships.

The constructs of formal and informal learning overlap with each other, and as Malcolm et al. (2003) asserted, there are significant elements of formal learning in informal learning contexts, and vice versa. They further argued: "It is important not to see informal and formal attributes as somehow separate, waiting to be integrated … for informal and formal attributes are present and interrelated" (p. 315). It is essential, therefore, to recognize and identify the different components of informal and formal learning to better understand their influences on learners, organizations, learning contexts, and outcomes. Further, formal and informal learning can frame mentoring relationships and opportunities within CPE.

Defining Mentoring

Numerous definitions of mentoring exist in the literature, varying because of the contexts in which the relationships occur and the types of mentoring attributes described, such as psychosocial support and/or career growth. In a seminal definition of mentoring that focused on career development, Kram (1985) described mentoring as an intense relationship between experienced colleagues working with less experienced persons to promote professional and/or psychosocial support and growth. Schunk and Mullen (2013) deepened the definition, declaring that mentoring involves "interactions between more-experienced mentors and less experienced protégés" (p. 362), where mentors may provide professional and psychological assistance and support to help mentees achieve career and personal achievements through long-term professional relationships that develop and deepen over time. Mentoring may also be "a complex intellectual, social, and emotional construct with the capacity for professional support, learning and professional knowledge within the context in which it is practiced and within broader societal norms and values" (Simmie & Moles, 2012, p. 109). Other definitions of mentoring take into account expanding types of mentoring relationships that occur in schools, workplaces, and professional organizations, such as comentoring, peer mentoring, and e-mentoring. Mentoring relationships in many different contexts have the potential to promote psychosocial development and career growth and critical reflection through transformational and other types of learning.

Informal and Formal Mentoring

Informal mentoring occurs when mentors and mentees agree to work together based on common understandings, interests, and goals. These relationships may be psychosocial in nature, providing learning support for mentees. They enhance self-esteem through the interpersonal dynamics of the relationships, the emotional bonds they form, and the work they accomplish together (Hansman, 2000, 2012). Informal mentoring includes mentees, and sometimes their mentors, engaging in peer mentoring groups formed through alliances among colleagues. Informal or psychosocial mentoring offers emotional support to enhance mentees' self-esteem and confidence and advance their careers. Psychosocial supports that mentors provide include role modeling, confirmation, counseling, and friendship (Hansman, 2000, 2001). Mentors can also guide mentees through career choices and protect them from hostile work contexts.

Formal Mentoring Programs. Formal mentoring programs are organized by workplaces or professional organizations to "answer management and organizational problems, such as accelerating the transfer of skills and knowledge pertinent to the organization, building teams, enhancing workforce diversity, implementing total quality management, and developing leadership skills" (Hansman, 2000, p. 496). Formal mentoring programs in workplaces, professional organizations, or CPE are also formed to preserve and promote cultures, create future leaders, reduce turnover, and fulfill organizational diversity goals. Formal mentoring programs can also be a vehicle for CPE to promote individual learning while building learning communities that enhance organizational learning and professional development.

Mentoring Relationships and Power. Formal mentoring programs may be problematic in several ways (Hansman, 2002). Studies (see Johnson-Bailey, 2012; Thomas, 2001) have indicated that discrimination may prevent mentees from engaging in helpful mentoring relationships; specifically, "Gender, race, class ethnicity, ability, sexual orientation, and issues of power may affect how mentees and mentors interact and negotiate their relationships" (Hansman, 2002, p. 40). Generational differences may also cause difficulties in forming mentoring relationships.

Acknowledged and unacknowledged power structures may also exist within formal and informal mentoring relationships. Ragins (1997) defined *power* as the "influence of one person over others, stemming from an individual characteristic, an interpersonal relationship, a position in an organization, or from membership in a societal group" (p. 485). Mentors typically have more power than their mentees in mentoring relationships through the positions they hold within organizations or professional networks. Their power may result in hierarchical paternalistic relationships where mentors make assumptions concerning what is best for their mentees. Mentors may further exercise power by not providing assistance to mentees in understanding and navigating the organizational politics that may support or impede their careers, or they may hinder their mentees from critically examining organizational values or structures that may privilege certain ways of knowing or groups over others. Ragins and Kram (2007) and Schunk and Mullen (2013) explored the concept of power–distance within mentoring relationships, with *high* power–distance manifesting into top-down authoritative relationships and *low* power–distance manifesting into encouraging collaborative and comentoring relationships.

Learning Through Mentoring in CPE

Both formal and informal mentoring relationships assist mentees to learn from and in everyday work practices, especially when mentoring relationships are situated in practice environments that are made more meaningful by the workplace or everyday contexts. Eraut (2004, 2007) asserted that mentoring may be considered informal learning, yet it is more formal than other learning processes in CPE. Eraut (2007) encouraged novices, mentors, and managers to understand the variety of ways people can learn in workplaces, discuss learning needs, and "recognize and attend to the factors which enhance or hinder individual learning" (p. 420).

Learning in CPE mentoring relationships is more than a transfer of knowledge. Instead, enriched mentoring relationships include mentors coaching mentees through career-related issues, sponsoring mentees in CPE settings, or assigning challenging work tasks to mentees to complete and to reflect upon for their learning, growth, and development. As Cervero (1992) has contended, the richest and most meaningful source of knowledge that professionals acquire is through everyday work life and reflections on tasks. Mentoring relationships may foster many different types of learning, including critical reflection and critical coconstructing of knowledge.

Critical Reflection. Critical reflection is:

A social learning process involving a great deal of peer learning. ... People come to a better understanding of their own assumptions and develop the ability to judge their accuracy and validity only if they involve peers as critically reflective mirrors who provide them with images of how their practice looks to others. (Brookfield, 2009, p. 133)

Cranton (2009) advances Brookfield's concepts, asserting that an essential element to critical reflection is to "expose individuals to alternative perspectives" (p. 185) through discussions and activities that are designed to encourage self-reflection as well as reflection within the group.

Through discourse and critical reflection, mentors and their mentees may examine past, current, and possible future experiences to further learning within practice contexts. "Unpacking" learning events or activities through discourse aids mentors and mentees to understand the unique needs of individuals within mentoring relationships so that additional developmental activities can be planned. Moreover, critical reflection may help foster psychosocial support as well as career learning and development among mentees and mentors.

Critical-Constructivist Perspective. Similar to the views of Daley and Cervero in Chapter 2, Crow (2012) has described learning from a critical-constructivist perspective, contending that learning "does not simply involve a transmission of knowledge. ... It involves the social construction of knowledge, in which knowledge is co-constructed through the social negotiation process of relationship" (p. 231). Examining formal and informal mentoring relationships from a critical-constructivist perspective allows for discourse concerning shared power and coconstruction of knowledge within mentoring relationships, permitting a "bottom-up culture of learning in organizations that is driven by the real and urgent needs of professionals" (de Laat & Schreurs, 2013, p. 1422).

Taking a critical-constructivist lens allows for challenges to "the organizational status quo" (Crow, 2012, p. 234) so that mentors and mentees can think about "narrow power relationships" where only one person (the mentor) in the relationship possesses power or expertise. Yet through honest and open dialogue, mentoring relationships have the potential to transform into a more balanced liaison, with mentors and mentees sharing power to engage in social and political negotiations where knowledge and learning are reciprocal. Learning within a constructivist or critical-constructivist perspective may facilitate both individual and group reflection on experiences (deGroot, Endedijk, Jaarsma, Simons, & van Beukelen, 2014), depending upon the mentoring context, while also involving learners in active learning, such as problem- or work-based learning exercises, creative activities, and critical reflections. Mentoring relationships that adopt a critical-constructivist perspective challenge organizational or professional goals and question whose interests are being privileged at the expense of others, perhaps opening the door for individual and/or organizational transformation.

Innovative Mentoring Relationship in Real World Practice: Two Contemporary Examples

Many professionals, such as lawyers and mental health counselors, are mandated to meet annual requirements for CPE, usually accomplished through engaging in seminars, writing projects, or other types of activities. The next section describes two examples of innovative CPE mentoring programs from the Law Society of British Columbia and the American Counseling

Association, proving that mentoring relationships can provide powerful learning opportunities in CPE programs.

Law Society of British Columbia Formalized Mentoring Program. As an example of CPE through a formalized mentoring program, the Law Society of British Columbia provides guidelines for mentoring among its members that enables them to earn continuing professional development credit (CPD). The Law Society of British Columbia (n.d.) has described mentoring as:

> A relationship in which a lawyer with experience or expertise in a practice area or practice skill (the "mentor") provides guidance or advice in support of the professional or practice goals of another lawyer, or an articling student in another firm, who requests assistance (the "mentee"). (para. 1)

To qualify as a mentor, a lawyer must have 7 to 10 years of practice in Canada and "need not be senior to the mentee, but must have sufficient experience or expertise in the subjects under discussion to enable the mentee to learn" (para. 2). To earn CPD credit, a mentoring plan must be approved by the Law Society of British Columbia with the mentee's specific development and learning goals complying with the same "categories of subject matter as required for any CPD credit" (para. 5), such as broad practice issues and skills but should not include business development, marketing, or wellness or work/life balance issues. Further requirements for CPD credit include mentors and mentees agreeing to meet in sessions of 30 minutes, totaling a minimum of at least 6 hours over the course of a year, to earn six CPD credits. A mentor lawyer must have expertise in the areas of learning discussed in the mentoring plan. The mentoring sessions can take place face to face, by phone, or through other electronic conferencing tools. At the conclusion of the mentoring sessions, mentors and mentees must document their sessions and submit their report to the society for CPD credit.

In a narrative description of their approved Law Society mentoring relationship, lawyers McDonnell and Pun (2012) discussed their relationship as "instructive, inspiring, and enjoyable" (p. 347). Prior to their participation in the mentoring program, McDonnell served as an informal mentor and role model to Pun. However, Pun sought to formalize their mentoring relationship as a means to accomplish some of his CPD credits while at the same time learning from McDonnell's experience and expertise in certain areas of the law. Pun also hoped to gain second-hand knowledge of the work of other well-known lawyers with whom McDonnell frequently associated and worked. They collaboratively developed a mentoring plan to include the topics of "hard law and practice," trial and appellate counsel, and expert evidence. Pun saw their relationship as a way to "discuss these matters with a trusted friend who might well bring a different perspective on any numbers of topics" (McDonnell & Pun, 2012, p. 342). In his role as mentor, McDonnell prepared papers, outlines, and case examples on which the mentor and mentee could reflect and discuss in their mentoring sessions. The pair met for four 2-hour sessions to fulfill their required 6 hours over the year. From his perspective as a mentee, Pun found the relationship to be beneficial and a valuable opportunity to develop professionally, and he plans on seeking other mentors for future professional development. As a mentor, McDonnell described learning as much as his mentee while fulfilling his role as a mentor because he "had to think through each subject from basic principles to its application in recent jurisprudence" (McDonnell & Pun, 2012, p. 344) while preparing for mentoring sessions. He also described how the questions and hypothetical situations posed by his mentee caused him to rethink approaches to topics and "make revisions on the fly ... just another way of saying I learned a lot" (McDonnell & Pun, 2012, p. 344).

Although it was formalized in a CPE program, the mentoring relationship described by McDonnell and Pun (2012) also included informal mentoring aspects. For example, despite adhering to the planned and Law Society approved subjects, the pair also recounted how they discussed personal issues and social matters in their meetings, conversations that served to enable them to understand each other better and to gain knowledge of other areas of their law practices. This informal aspects of their relationship increased their collegiality and respect for each other and the professional work each did. In the future, it might be helpful to mentors and mentees to enlarge the list of allowed topics to include personal as well as professional foci so that a stronger and more personal relationship might be established.

American Counseling Association: Supporting Professional Identity Development Through Mentoring. The American Counseling Association (2016) standards emphasize professional identity development and the professional roles of counselors and professional counseling organizations (Kaplan & Gladding, 2011). Viewing identity development and professional learning as intertwined (Dirkx, 2013) leads to a consideration of the integration between personal and professional selves that begins in counselors' preservice training and continues throughout their professional careers.

In the context of counseling, Murdock, Stipanovic, and Lucas (2013) developed a comentoring program to address identity development, pairing master's-level counselors with doctoral counseling students to advance their understandings of professional practice and identity. Murdock et al. chose comentoring because it "can be traced to a feminist perspective and is credited with reducing power differences and providing those within the relationship with a sense of equality, allowing both to draw upon one another's strengths" (p. 491). In the comentoring program, doctoral students, as more experienced members, were paired with master's students with the goal to:

> Provide the other with experiences that would aid their professional identity development, with the master's students receiving experiences to aid in their professional identity as practitioners, and doctoral students receiving experiences

to aid in their professional identity as future faculty members and/or clinical supervisors. (Murdock et al., 2013, p. 491)

Murdock et al. coached the mentors to develop lists of suggested topics to address in the comentoring relationships, such as traversing graduate school; planning coursework and related issues; developing research projects, thesis, and conference presentations; joining professional organizations at local and national levels; and applying to doctoral programs. Comentors were mandated to meet a minimum of four times during the semester, and to encourage continual communication, a written communication component was integrated in which comentors exchanged email and/or written letters at least eight times over the semester to strengthen their relationships between face-to-face meetings.

In researching the effectiveness of this program, Murdock et al. (2013) discovered that the participants experienced "enhanced professional identity development and collegial professional relationships" (p. 487). The comentoring program heightened the master's students' personal growth and identities as professional counselors and their mindfulness of the differing cultural aspects of participants and professional settings. The doctoral comentors furthered their professional development through the challenges of mentoring less experienced counselors. They also explored the similarities between comentoring others and the counseling process through their participation in collegial relationships and friendships that allowed them to "give back" to others through providing guidance and support. In short, comentoring structures allowed for nonhierarchical helpful relationships to develop between the participants and reduced power differentials that may be present among mentors and mentees in mentoring relationships.

Conclusion

I began this chapter with a metaphor for mentoring relationships, with a more experienced mentor "sending the elevator down" to bring mentees "up" to help them in their personal and professional growth and development. The two examples of mentoring relationships discussed are examples of empowered mentoring relationships in which power differentials are mitigated by collaboratively planning ways to share knowledge and engage in experiential learning activities. In this way, learning may "not be controlled by corporate curriculum agenda, relying on outside experts and outside sources of knowledge" (de Laat & Schreurs, 2013, p. 1422); instead, knowledge is negotiated and coconstructed among mentors and mentees. To continue the metaphor, elevators are sent down with mentors and mentees riding together in them to plan and carry out constructive and collaborative mentoring relationships. Mentees are not made to climb the steps, but are elevated in their professional growth in upward-bound elevators—supportive and powerful relationships that promote professional learning and development within CPE.

References

American Counseling Association. (2016). *20/20: Principles for unifying and strengthening the profession*. Retrieved from http://www.counseling.org/knowledge-center/20-20-a-vision-for-the-future-of-counseling/statement-of-principles.

Brookfield, S. (2009). Engaging critical reflection in corporate America. In J. Mezirow, E. Taylor, & Associates (Eds.), *Transformative learning in practice: Insights from community, workplace and higher education* (pp. 125–135). San Francisco, CA: Jossey-Bass.

Cervero, R. (1992). Professional practice, learning, and continuing education: An integrated perspective. *International Journal of Lifelong Education, 11*(2), 91–101.

Cranton, P. (2009). From tradesperson to teacher: A transformative transition. In J. Mezirow, E. Taylor, & Associates (Eds.), *Transformative learning in practice: Insights from community, workplace and higher education* (pp. 182–192). San Francisco, CA: Jossey-Bass.

Colley, H., Hodkinson, H., & Malcolm, J. (2003). Understanding informality and formality in learning. *Adults Learning, 15*(3), 7–9.

Crow, G. (2012). A critical-constructivist perspective on mentoring and coaching for leadership. In S. Fletcher & C. Mullen (Eds.), *The Sage handbook of mentoring and coaching in education* (pp. 228–242). London, UK: Sage.

deGroot, E., Endedijk, M., Jaarsma, D., Simons, P., & van Beukelen, P. (2014). Critically reflective dialogues in learning communities of professionals. *Studies in Continuing Education, 36*(1), 15–37. doi:10.1080/0158037X.2013.779240

de Laat, M., & Schreurs, B. (2013). Visualizing informal professional development networks: Building a case for learning analytics in the workplace. *American Behavioral Scientist, 57*(10), 1421–1438. doi:10.1177/0002764213479364

Dirkx, J. (2013). Leaning in and leaning back at the same time: Toward spirituality of work-related learning. *Advances in Developing Human Resources, 15*(4), 356–369. doi:10.1177/1523422313498562

Eraut, M. (2004). Informal learning in the workplace. *Studies in Continuing Education, 26*(2), 247–273. doi:10.1080/158037042000225245

Eraut, M. (2007). Learning from other people in the workplace. *Oxford Review of Education, 33*(4), 403–422. doi:10.1080/03054980701425706

Hansman, C. (2000) Formal mentoring programs. In A. Wilson & E. Hayes (Eds.), *Handbook of adult and continuing education* (pp. 493–507). San Francisco, CA: Jossey-Bass.

Hansman, C. (2001). Mentoring as continuing professional education. *Adult Learning, 12*, 7–8.

Hansman, C. (2002). Diversity and power in mentoring relationships. In C. Hansman (Ed.), *Critical perspectives on mentoring: Trends and issues* (Information Series No. 388, pp. 39–48). Columbus, OH: ERIC Clearinghouse on Adult, Career, and Vocational Education. (ED465045)

Hansman, C. (2012). Empowerment in the faculty-student mentoring relationship. In C. Mullen & S. Fletcher (Eds.), *Handbook of mentoring and coaching in education* (pp. 368–382). London, UK: Sage.

Houle, C. O (1980) *Continuing learning in the professions*. San Francisco, CA: Jossey-Bass.

Johnson-Bailey, J. (2012). Effects of race and racial dynamics on mentoring. In S. Fletcher & C. Mullen (Eds.), *The Sage handbook of mentoring and coaching in education* (pp. 155–168). London, UK: Sage.

Kaplan, D. M., & Gladding, S. (2011). A vision for the future of counseling: The 20/20 principles for unifying and strengthening the profession. *Journal of Counseling & Development, 89*, 267–272.

Katsir, J., & Moreschi, O. (Writers). (2015, September 16). *The Late Show with Stephen Colbert* [Television series]. Spartina Productions & CBS Television Studios (Producers). New York, NY: CBS.

Kram, K. (1985). *Mentoring at work: Developmental relationships in organizational life*. Glenview, IL: Scott, Foresman & Company.

Law Society of British Columbia (n.d.). *Continuing professional development: Mentoring*. Retrieved from http://www.lawsociety.bc.ca/page.cfm?cid=262&t=Mentoring.

Malcolm, J., Hodkinson, P., & Colley, H. (2003). The interrelationships between informal and formal learning. *Journal of Workplace Learning, 15*(7/8), 313–318.

McDonnell, Q., & Pun, G. (2012). Mentoring and continuing professional development. *The Advocate, 7*(3), 341–347.

Mullen, C. (2012). Mentoring: An overview. In C. Mullen & S. Fletcher (Eds.), *Handbook of mentoring and coaching in education* (pp. 7–23). London, UK: Sage.

Murdock, J., Stipanovic, N., & Lucas, K. (2013). Fostering connections between graduate students and strengthening professional identity through co-mentoring. *British Journal of Guidance & Counselling, 41*(5), 4897–4903.

Queeney, D. S. (2000). Continuing professional education. In A. Wilson & E. Hayes (Eds.), *Handbook of adult and continuing education* (pp. 375–391). San Francisco, CA: Jossey-Bass.

Ragins, B. (1997). Diversified mentoring relationships in organizations: A power perspective. *Academy of Management Review, 22*(2), 485–521.

Ragins, B., & Kram, K. (2007). *The handbook of mentoring at work: Theory, research, and practice*. Thousand Oaks, CA: Sage.

Sandlin, J., Wright, R., & Clark, C. (2011). Re-examining theories of adult learning and adult development through the lenses of public pedagogy. *Adult Education Quarterly, 6*(1), 3–23.

Schunk, D., & Mullen, C. (2013). Toward a conceptual model of mentoring research: Integration with self-regulated learning. *Educational Psychology Review, 25*, 361–389. doi:10.1007/s10648-013-9233-3

Simmie, G., & Moles, J. (2012). Educating the critically reflective mentor. In C. Mullen & S. Fletcher (Eds.), *Handbook of mentoring and coaching in education* (pp. 107–121). London, UK: Sage.

Thomas, D. (2001). The truth about mentoring minorities: Race matters. *Harvard Business Review, 79*(4), 99–107.

CATHERINE A. HANSMAN *is professor of Adult Learning and Development and director of the Master of Education in Health Professions Education at Cleveland State University, Cleveland, Ohio.*

In this chapter, the author explores a variety of aspects of continuing professional education for teachers and university and college faculty members. She discusses the kinds of knowledge that are addressed and the role of online learning in continuing professional education.

Continuing Professional Education for Teachers and University and College Faculty

Patricia Cranton

Most things we learn involve different kinds of knowledge—instrumental or technical, communicative, and emancipatory (Habermas, 1971). I think of the visual artist or the musician who needs the foundations of technique and skill before he or she can produce works that connect with audiences or the writer of fiction who needs to know how to construct a good story. I also think of the teacher who needs to know how to organize a course outline, create instructional materials, and not talk to a class with her or his back to the group.

For many years, I taught in the Instructional Development Program, offered by the University of New Brunswick in Canada for community college instructors. The program was mandatory for any instructor going into a full-time teaching position in the college system. The participants were mostly tradespeople learning how to be teachers of their trades. They had not been in a university environment before, and most were feeling vulnerable and anxious. They wanted the "nuts and bolts" of teaching: how to do things, that is, instrumental and technical knowledge. The program needed to supply that; otherwise, we could not have gone any further with the learning. But we could not end there. We needed to go on to the different kinds of learning required in continuing professional education. The challenge was to make the transition from the technical to the communicative and emancipatory in a way that was meaningful for the participants.

In this chapter, I provide a brief overview of the different kinds of knowledge and then discuss professional and faculty development as a subset of continuing professional education, including the emphasis on technical and instrumental knowledge in professional development. I explore the role of power in this model of professional development and look at alternative perspectives. I briefly put this discussion within the framework of informal, nonformal, and

NEW DIRECTIONS FOR ADULT AND CONTINUING EDUCATION, no. 151, Fall 2016 © 2016 Wiley Periodicals, Inc.
Published online in Wiley Online Library (wileyonlinelibrary.com) • DOI: 10.1002/ace.20194

formal learning. Given the increasing demand for online professional development, I then go on to describe the online learning context and how to facilitate online professional development.

Continuing Professional Education, Professional Development, and Faculty Development

The terminology can become confusing. Continuing professional education is the more general, umbrella term that includes formal programs and non-formal and informal learning for people in all of the professions. This is the term that is most often used in the adult education literature; therefore, it is the term used most frequently in this chapter. Professional development is usually used to describe K–12 teachers' professional development. The term faculty development refers to programs and nonformal learning for college and university faculty. Although these terms are often viewed as separate disciplines with literatures that do not intersect, the concerns and issues in these fields are very similar. I have practiced in each of these areas (more so in faculty development and professional development for teachers), but when I worked in faculty development at McGill University (for 10 years), the majority of the participants were faculty colleagues from medicine, nursing, dentistry, and physical therapy. They also had continuing professional education programs in their discipline that operated independently of learning about teaching. What I came to see is that all three of these groups share common concerns. They are interested in how to improve their curriculum, how to increase their teaching effectiveness, how to assess their teaching effectiveness, and how to expand their students' learning beyond the basic instrumental knowledge in the field.

Kinds of Knowledge

Instrumental knowledge is that which allows us to manipulate and control the environment, predict observable physical and social events, and take appropriate actions. Empirical or natural scientific methodologies produce technically useful knowledge, the knowledge necessary for industry and production in modern society. Knowledge is established by reference to external reality, using the senses. In this perspective, there is an objective world made up of observable phenomena. The laws governing physical and social systems can be identified through science, and these systems are seen to operate independently of human perceptions.

The second kind of knowledge is based on our need to understand each other through language. Habermas (1971) calls this practical or *communicative* knowledge. Human beings have always been social creatures, instinctively forming groups, tribes, communities, cultures, and nations in order to satisfy their mutual needs. In order for people to survive together in groups and societies, they must communicate with and understand each other. There are

New Directions for Adult and Continuing Education • DOI: 10.1002/ace

no scientific laws governing these communications; when we communicate with others, we interpret what they say in our own way. All societies share and transmit social knowledge, that is, a code of commonly accepted beliefs and behavior. As a society we come to agree on how things should be and are in reference to standards and values, moral and political issues, educational and social systems, and government actions.

The third kind of knowledge, which derives from a questioning of both instrumental and communicative knowledge, Habermas calls *emancipatory* knowledge. By nature, people are interested in self-knowledge, growth, development, and freedom. Gaining emancipatory knowledge is dependent on our abilities to be self-determining and self-reflective. Self-determination can be described as the capacity to both be aware of and critical of ourselves and of our social and cultural context. Self-reflection involves being aware of and critical of our subjective perceptions of knowledge and of the constraints of social knowledge.

All three kinds of knowledge are a part of continuing professional education, teacher professional development, and faculty development. In the next section, I discuss the three kinds of knowledge in relation to continuing professional education. Because the leader of programs is often an adult educator, and because the participants are usually also educators (including adult educators), the terminology can be confusing. The term "provider" tends to imply a teacher-directed way of working with learners (the teacher provides the information), so though I may use the word "provider" where it is appropriate, I choose to use the term "facilitator" and describe the learners as "participants" so as to emphasize the importance of having a learner-centered approach to continuing professional education.

The Emphasis on Technical and Instrumental Knowledge

For a teacher learning how to teach or how to improve his or her teaching, the focus is sometimes on technical and instrumental knowledge. The goals can be clearly defined and the teaching methods can focus on the goals. There is little give-and-take in this kind of professional development as the goal is to give participants the skills they need, often just to cope with the entry stages of their professional practice (for example, how to create clear objectives for a course, how to develop PowerPoint presentations). Teachers in continuing professional education programs often want to acquire technical skills, so there is a match between what they want and what the program providers are able to do. This is likely, in part, why the majority of continuing professional education programs for educators in formal contexts emphasize technical knowledge about teaching (Cranton, 2005).

Anyone who teaches, and anyone who teaches teachers, knows full well that though technical knowledge is necessary, just as it is for the artist or the musician, it is only one layer of what they need to know. Teachers need to be concerned with communicative knowledge as learning how to teach is concerned with the understanding of social norms and the understanding of individuals within social structures. Communicative knowledge is socially constructed in groups through dialogue, shared experiences, and exchanges of resources and ideas. I discuss this in more detail in the next section.

But first, I think it is important to realize that the model of technical knowledge as continuing professional education says a lot about power. Technical knowledge is based on the idea that there is an objective reality. There is "true" knowledge, and authorities possess that knowledge. So in continuing professional education, the educator who focuses on technical knowledge is the person who is in control. This is fine if it is one aspect of a program, but it is not so fine if it comprises an entire program. The person who owns this knowledge is the authority and has the power of that knowledge (Brookfield, 2006; English, 2006).

Communicative and Emancipatory Knowledge

When communicative and emancipatory knowledge are a part of continuing professional education, the facilitator (or provider) and the participants are more likely to share power. Colearning, emancipatory learning, experiential learning, and socially constructed learning all involve power sharing. The facilitator guides, and contributes resources, but she or he is not the ultimate authority, and she is not the one to tell people what to do. The participants in continuing professional education programs have experience and knowledge in their field, and they often have quite a lot of knowledge about how to teach in their subject area. The facilitator builds on what the participants know and becomes a colearner with them.

I am currently teaching several online courses for teachers, courses that serve as continuing professional education for the participants. Although I have been doing this for decades, I keep experimenting with letting go of my authority in order to become a better colearner. In my current course, I turned some of the forums completely over to the participants. "It's your turn," I posted. "This forum is yours." I asked them to pose the discussion questions, construct activities, and take charge of the forums. The participants respond enthusiastically. Since I started doing this, the number of posts has doubled in one course, tripled in another.

Then an interesting thing happened. I responded to their activities and discussion questions as though I were an enrolled student. But almost no one responded to me in that role. I think two or three students (out of 50) responded to my posts. To me, this shows how strong the power issues are, even though I have generally have good relationships with the participants. They appreciate my comments and responses to their posts, but they simply did not know what to do with me when I was acting as a peer.

This takes me to brief discussion of informal, nonformal, and formal learning. From there, I explore online learning as a vehicle for continuing professional education.

Informal, Nonformal, and Formal Learning

A great deal of continuing professional education for teachers, faculty, and professionals is nonformal. That is, it consists of workshops, discussion groups, and other activities that are not completed for credit but are organized. Informal professional development includes the conversations among faculty, the exchange of resources among educators, the reading of journals, and all activities that are not associated with any formal or nonformal activities. And formal learning is that which takes place in the context of institutions' programs (certificates, degrees, and continuing education activities).

Formal learning in continuing professional education has been growing exponentially through the availability of online learning. It is not only certificate programs, but also master's of education programs that are now offered fully online for educators looking for programs to advance their learning and their practice. We need to pay a lot of attention to the role of online learning and to understand how best to facilitate this kind of learning. It is not a matter of simply transferring existing courses to an online platform, and it is especially not a matter of continuing with the transmission of technical knowledge in a different medium.

Online Learning in Continuing Professional Education

Continuing professional development education relies on a collaborative environment where participants exchange ideas and socially construct knowledge in their profession. In an online context, my challenge is to create this collaborative learning environment (Cranton, 2010). We know that face-to-face courses cannot simply be transferred to an online environment; we need to take into account the important differences between face-to-face teaching and online teaching, but we know little about how collaboration can be encouraged successfully online.

In writing about fostering transformative learning online, I suggest several strategies to foster collaboration (Cranton, 2010). I bring in the voices from the participants in my online courses to support my suggestions. Because transformative learning relies in large part on collaboration among individuals, many of these strategies are relevant to our discussion here. There is evidence that learners are more likely to be open in their communications with their peers online than they are in a face-to-face setting, a phenomenon that I like to call "the stranger-on-the-train" phenomenon. It can be easier to talk to people that we do not see and will not meet. Online discussions remain accessible and do not disappear the moment after they occur, as they do in face-to-face learning; there is time for reflection and contemplation. Links to resources are immediately available rather than something that students need to look up after a class meeting. In addition, the adult educators' presence in online learning can support both relationships with individuals and with the group with ease,

New Directions for Adult and Continuing Education • DOI: 10.1002/ace

whereas in face-to-face learning, the educator cannot as easily connect to all individuals within a group.

Inviting learners' input into the topics for the course sets the stage for collaborative learning; participants feel involved and valued, and they see that their interests in topics are shared with others in the group. If the facilitator encourages discussions among participants rather than hosting a series of question-and-answer interactions with individuals in the group, students will move quickly into engaging each other with ideas, stories about their experiences, and questions about each other's perspectives. The adult educator needs to walk a fine line between being clearly present in an online course and dominating the discussion. For example, he or she should make sure to respond to each individual in any one discussion forum, but not to respond to all postings and especially not to those postings addressed to other group members. This balancing act takes some practice, and it also needs to be flexible.

Strategies for Creating Collaborative Learning Online

Although he was not writing about online learning, Wlodkowski (2008) gives us concrete guidelines and strategies for helping diverse groups of people learn well together—strategies that make a considerable sense in our now-global approach to online learning. He explores the concept of motivation and "discusses the core characteristics ... that are necessary for a person to be a motivating instructor" (p. xiii). He provides illustrations of how to create a motivational framework and how to develop goal from this framework: establishing inclusion (respect and connectedness), developing attitude (self-determination and relevance), enhancing meaning, (engagement and challenge) and engendering competence (authenticity and effectiveness). Each of these facets of Wlodkowski's motivational framework can inform the work of online adult educators who strive to create an environment conducive to collaborative learning.

Colearning Online for Professional Development

In continuing professional education, the educator and the learners may come from the same environment and have a shared idea of what being an educator in their field means. When this is the case, rather than the educator assuming the role of authority, he or she can be a colearner working with other professionals in the same field. This moves the power relations away from the educator into a domain where power is shared. Both the educator and the participants can determine together the path that the learning will take.

In an online environment, this is a little more difficult to navigate than it is in a face-to-face environment. I have struggled with how to implement this. When I simply post, "Please tell us what you would like to learn in the next weeks of the course," the responses are hesitant or nonexistent. Based on their prior experiences, participants are reluctant to believe that they may actually have a say in the course. "It is the job of the teacher to organize the course," is the message conveyed. What I have worked out over the years is to approach this in a gradual way. I no longer ask participants to directly indicate what they want to learn. During the first week of the course, I focus on creating a learning community. For the next 2 weeks or so, I post the topic for the discussion forum. Then, I move into giving participants choices and inviting them to participate in decision making about the course. I try to create an environment where choice and decision making are a natural part of how the course progresses. I always give a choice in every discussion forum. "Please do 'this' or 'that.'" I also emphasize that anyone at any time can create her or his alternative way of approaching the topic at hand.

Self-Evaluation Online

Here is a crunch. When continuing professional education for professional development is held in formal settings, evaluation of student learning is usually controlled or prescribed by the providing institution (e.g., professional associations and licensing bodies). Yet, I strongly believe that student self-evaluation is central to the process of professional development. As professionals, we need to be able to assess our strengths, and we need to be able to evaluate what we do and learn. That is a part of what it means to be professional.

What I do is ask the participants in my course to send me a one-page self-evaluation in which they give me the grade that reflects their learning in all aspects of the course. I accept their grade and record it without question. But in my course description, all I say is, "You will be asked to participate in the evaluation of your learning." [As Newman (2006) says, teaching is a subversive activity.]

An Illustration: Fostering Professional Continuing Education Online

Here, I focus on one online course that I am currently teaching, which is typical of the formal professional development options for teachers. The course is a "how to teach" course, but it focuses on becoming an authentic teacher, a topic that includes self-awareness exercises, critical reflection, sharing stories, and exploring the meaning of authenticity in a context where there are so many constraints to teaching imposed by the educational systems, especially mandatory curriculum, standardized testing, outcomes-based assessment, and the like. The course explores instrumental and technical knowledge as it is raised by the participants, and sometimes a discussion forum focuses mainly on technical knowledge at the request of the teachers in the course. More often, though, it focuses on shared values and beliefs, and during those discussions, participants very often see things from a different perspective (and experience emancipatory learning).

I facilitate two sections of this course, with 20 participants in each. The participants are almost all elementary, middle school, and high school teachers, but there are a few (less than five) adult educators working in organizations or the health professions. All of the participants are taking the course as a professional development activity. They work full time and take courses part time. They may receive a pay increase or be seeking promotion to an administrative position, but this is not their primary motivation in taking the courses.

I take one full week at the beginning of a 12-week course to develop a learning community. There is no reference to the content of the course during this first week. I do not have a traditional syllabus with its long list of expectations and readings, but rather a simple course schedule, which is flexible and open to change as we go. During the initial week, participants talk about who they are and where they teach. They tell us about their families and pets and backgrounds. We often end up exchanging photographs of dogs and children. Most participants are from New Brunswick, Canada, which has a family-oriented culture. People explore how they know the same people and who is related to whom. Even though I cannot see the participants, I can feel them relax and I can hear them thinking, "This is not so bad, I can do this."

For one more week, we pay no attention to the course text. We discuss what authenticity means to us, in any sense. What is an authentic work of art? What is authentic text? Who is an authentic person? By now, there are about 200 posts from 20 students in each section. I think this kind of introduction to professional development (either online or in person) brings people together and takes them away from the anxiety-provoking idea of engaging in online learning. It is usually not until midway through the course when someone thinks to ask how many postings I am expecting them to do. And this is a good opportunity to comment on educator power. We have interesting and complicated discussions about educator power. Teachers in the public school system are more constrained by their context than is anyone in adult or higher education. We end up exploring power relations and the context of teachers' practice. I question the participants, and they question each other. We don't always agree, of course. But our discussions are provocative. Sometimes, I find myself feeling frustrated. How can they believe this stuff that they are told by their principals? How can they support outcomes-based assessment?

I develop relationships with the participants. Not always with everyone, of course. But with many. It is not easy to describe how this works. I focus on someone who seems to be anxious or lacking in self-confidence. I make sure to respond to that person. Or, I notice when I have not responded to an individual for a few days, and I make sure to do so. I often make a connection through a common interest that I might have with a participant. But, and this is especially interesting in a course about authenticity in teaching, I have learned that the students do not especially want to know anything about me. I used to try to be "myself" in my responses to students and tell some story that was relevant to the topic under discussion, but it did not take me long to realize that no one responded to this, so I stopped doing it. I now focus on the students. I talk about what they have posted.

Listening and questioning are central to working with participants online. I realize that many online courses do not have a strong educator presence, but this is disturbing in the realm of professional development (and probably elsewhere). We learn through dialogue and exchanges of experiences. Learning is often, but not always, socially constructed. We need to pay attention to this in online professional education and in-person professional education.

Summary

Continuing professional education for teachers most often consists of one-time workshops or presentations by "experts" who bring a new set of resources or a new teaching strategy to the participants. Teachers feel frustrated by this for a variety of reasons. Presentations often come from individuals who are not practicing teachers and may not understand the daily life of a teacher. I realize that I could fall into this category, but I work so much with teachers and pay a lot of attention to what they say, so I hope I have more of an understanding of their practice than most. I see myself as a colearner, and they tend to view me this way as well.

Continuing professional education for faculty at colleges and universities has its own problems, beginning with the fact that it is almost always voluntary. This is a good thing, except that it also means that the majority of faculty members do not participate. Professional development activities are usually nonformal workshops, discussion groups, and one-on-one consultation with a faculty developer.

Continuing professional education for teachers and for faculty members tends to focus on techniques and strategies, without ever moving into the domains of communicative or emancipatory knowledge. This is a problem as learning about teaching involves communicative and emancipatory knowledge.

Teachers often turn to formal learning—certificates and graduate studies—for a more comprehensive approach to improving their practice. This is where they are likely to encounter online learning. Online programs for teachers are now plentiful. But it is essential that online formal learning for teachers goes beyond technical learning, and, unfortunately, it does not always do so. Access to online professional development for faculty members is less common.

I close the chapter with an illustration from my own practice with an online formal professional development course for teachers. The course focuses on establishing a learning community, developing relationships with students, and being present in the online environment. It seems that all of continuing professional education has something to learn from the recent developments in online learning. Teaching is a specialized form of communication where the goal is to foster learning and development. As such, learning about teaching needs to pay particular attention to communicative and collaborative learning. Ideally, it also needs to pay attention to emancipatory learning, where teachers in all contexts (K–12 and higher education) learn how to engage in critical questioning of their practice. Collaboration among adult educators across the various levels of education could go a long way toward meeting this goal.

References

Brookfield, S. S. (2006). Authenticity and power. In P. Cranton (Ed.), *New Directions for Adult and Continuing Education: No. 111. Authenticity in teaching* (pp. 5–16), San Francisco, CA: Jossey-Bass.

Cranton, P. (2005). Not making or shaping: Finding authenticity in faculty development. In S. Chadwick-Blossey (Ed.), *To improve the academy* (Vol. 24, pp. 70–85). San Francisco, CA: Jossey-Bass.

Cranton, P. (2010). Transformative learning in an online environment. *International Journal of Adult Vocational Education and Technology, 1*(2), 1–9.

English, L. M. (2006). Women, knowing, and authenticity: Living with contradictions. In P. Cranton (Ed.), *New Directions for Adult and Continuing Education: No. 111. Authenticity in teaching* (pp. 17–26). San Francisco, CA: Jossey-Bass.

Habermas, J. (1971). *Knowledge and human interests*. Boston: Beacon Press.

Newman, M. (2006). *Teaching defiance: Stories and strategies for activist educators*. San Francisco, CA: Jossey-Bass.

Wlodkowski, R. J. (2008). *Enhancing adult motivation to learn: A comprehensive guide for teaching all adults*. San Francisco, CA: Jossey-Bass.

PATRICIA CRANTON *is a retired professor of adult education affiliated with the University of New Brunswick. Her most recent books include* Stories of Transformative Learning, *with Michael Kroth (2015);* A Guide to Research for Educators and Trainers of Adults, *with Sharan Merriam, (2015); and* Measuring and Analyzing Informal Learning in the Digital Age, *coedited with Olutoyin Mejiuni and Olufemi Taiwo (2015). Patricia was inducted into the International Adult and Continuing Education Hall of Fame in 2014, and she was awarded the Order of Canada in 2016.*

5

*This chapter critiques the current state of CPE and offers and alternative
conceptualization of how CPE might be designed and delivered.*

Navigating Professional White Water:
Rethinking Continuing Professional
Education at Work

Laura L. Bierema

Today it is common to find professionals such as lawyers, doctors, or dentists
working in corporations as their services become commercialized:

> More professionals are becoming corporate full-time employees through the
> commercializing of such services as dentistry or corporations hiring lawyers to
> run human resource departments because the legal credential acts as a proxy for
> other skills or because legal skills are required by the organization for internal
> consulting. (Van Loo & Rocco, 2006, p. 203)

Professionals working in corporate settings not only experience learning provided by the organization but also face profession-mandated continuing professional education (CPE). This phenomenon puts human resource development (HRD) practitioners in the tenuous position of managing and facilitating
CPE with little control over the content, quality, or outcomes because CPE is
required and regulated by externalities such as professional associations (Van
Loo & Rocco, 2006).

Professionals train for years to become experts. Yet, gaps between their
education and the practice realities widen with globalization, technological advances, market competition, and knowledge development. Educational
interventions are necessary to keep professionals current. CPE is a recognized
intervention for addressing these gaps and equipping professionals with up-to-
date information and opportunities to refresh knowledge and skills that will
result in improved quality of professional services. CPE is integral to maintaining standards of quality and service in contemporary, constantly changing disciplines. Yet, there is increasing global cynicism about CPE's effectiveness, relevance, and sustainability. Much of CPE exists to comply with federal
and state requirements for licensure, certification, or practice (Jeris & Conway,

NEW DIRECTIONS FOR ADULT AND CONTINUING EDUCATION, no. 151, Fall 2016 © 2016 Wiley Periodicals, Inc.
Published online in Wiley Online Library (wileyonlinelibrary.com) • DOI: 10.1002/ace.20195

2003; Queeney, 2000). Yet, building, sustaining, and changing professions is a more dynamic process than minimum standards dictate, particularly when CPE occurs within organizational context.

Nicolaides (2015) suggested that we live in a complex time characterized by "liquid modernity" (p. 1). Liquid modernity refers to the fluidity of life where highly interconnected and interdependent professionals struggle to keep pace with relentless change and unpredictable outcomes. Nicolaides proposed that this fluidity creates ambiguity. She defined ambiguity as "an encounter with an appearance of reality that is at first unrecognizable, oblique, simultaneously evoking fear of "no-cognition" and the potential hope for multiple meanings irresolvable by reference to context alone" (p. 1).

Professionals must learn to cope with this ambiguity by "being flexible, adaptable, and constantly ready and willing to change tactics; to abandon commitments and loyalties without regret; and to act in a moment, as failure to act brings greater insecurity—such demands place adults 'in over their heads'" (Nicolaides, p. 2). Professional life breeds ambiguity with constantly changing regulations, players, and context. The professions are affected by this phenomenon of change that shifts form like water as they are pressured to offer improved and cheaper services, keep pace with technology, respond to regulations, and stay relevant within a globally competitive context. This time of "liquid modernity" (Nicolaides) echoes Vaill's (1996) metaphor of "permanent white water" representing the constant churn and turbulence typical of contemporary organizational life. Vaill advocated embracing "learning as a way of being" as key to navigating the choppy waters of organization life. Kegan (1995)suggested that we are "in over our heads" in our efforts to meet the mental demands of life and work. Clearly the challenges of learning in work context are roiling and changing.

The purpose of this chapter is to examine CPE from an organizational and workplace learning perspective, offer critiques of practice, and recommend alternatives to the current delivery and focus of CPE. Professional practice is located in organizations and communities, yet CPE tends to address learning needs and professionals in a vacuum with little regard for the social context of professional practice. The chapter profiles critical debates about CPE and calls for rethinking CPE that is more relevant in our current organizational and workplace contexts.

Defining CPE

CPE certifies and improves professional practice (Van Loo & Rocco, 2006). CPE's definitions range from instrumentalist, functionalist views that focus on improving professional knowledge, competence, and performance to critical views that focus on bettering society by improving access, equality, and reducing marginalization and oppression. The *continuing* in CPE represents the ceaseless need for professionals to sustain learning and maintain personal and

New Directions for Adult and Continuing Education • DOI: 10.1002/ace

professional competence. Given the current professional and global context, all stakeholders—individuals, organizations, associations, and CPE providers—need to develop educational cultures that support continuous retraining, educational opportunities and exposure to new ideas, processes, and technology (Balan, 2005). Continuing also assumes that professionals' development extends beyond their initial training resulting in successive career progression. Further, the continuing nature of CPE evolves from the assumption that professional training is necessary but not sufficient to ensure optional professional practice. Finally, continuing represents the constant churn of contemporary life that bombards professionals with massive information making it difficult to discern what is important to learn and change in professional practice.

The *professional* in CPE identifies an individual who practices a profession—an occupation populated by experts with specialized training, skills, and knowledge that are of benefit to society and controlled by institutions such as professional organizations that provide certification and/or licensure. Cervero (1988) categorized professions as service-oriented or community-oriented occupations that apply an expert body of knowledge to problems that society values as highly relevant, for example, education or health care. "Professionals define social problems with which they deal and by extension, actually define social needs" (Sleezer, Conti, & Nolan, 2004, p. 22). Bierema and Eraut (2004) identified three distinctive features characterizing professionals: (a) a body of formal knowledge acquired through professional and continuing education, (b) authoritative knowledge based on specialized knowledge and expertise, and (c) accountability to their clients through adherence to a professional code of conduct, which normally covers both ethical principles and obligations to maintain competence through ongoing learning. Professionals are required to demonstrate ongoing proficiency and competence with their training, skill and knowledge. CPE is sought in a world where knowledge is becoming obsolete as quickly as it is generated by new research and scholarship, requiring professionals to constantly update their toolbox.

Education implies a process of learning, development, and growth that is ongoing across the life span and expected if professionals are to keep pace with changes in knowledge and practice. CPE involves formal professional education that is relevant to practice. It may or may not lead to further credentialing and can be formal or informal, including clinical skills and professional issues (Jeris, 2010). Although defining CPE is rather straightforward, evaluating it is complicated (Clark, Draper, & Rogers, 2015; Eraut, 1985; Goodall, Day, Lindsay, Muijs, & Harris, 2005), its impact on practice is unclear (Cotterill-Walker, 2012; Lahti, Kontio, Pitkanen, & Valimaki, 2014), and what makes it effective is not well understood (Grant, 2011). The next section considers key critiques of CPE.

Critiques of CPE. CPE has existed since at least the Middle Ages (Houle, 1980) and today most occupations value continued learning as a key process of employment (Dirkx, Gilley, & Gilley, 2004). Houle's critique was that CPE participation rate carried no guarantee that improvements in competence or performance followed. Wessels (2007) argued that evidence of CPE's effectiveness is scant and that several factors limited its effectiveness such as cost, work constraints, family pressures, personal attitudes, or institutional barriers. Key problems with today's CPE are its update orientation, individualistic focus, instrumentality, relevance and effectiveness, and the resulting inattention to learning and the fluid, ambiguous, shifting environment of professional practice. Jeris and Daley (2004) noted in looking at CPE/HRD that shared areas of struggle included "the traditions of updating, weak links to performance, the isolation of learning from the workplace, and insufficient attention of research to the concept of learning" (p. 104).

Updating Versus Innovating. Continuing professional education has long been based on the update model (Nowlen, 1988) that involves learning and change at the individual level with little regard for particular work or social context (Dirkx, Gilley, & Gilley, 2004; Wilson & Cervero, 2014). CPE has ignored the complex relationships that profoundly affect learning and CPE (Dirkx, Gilley, & Gilley, 2004; Wilson & Cervero, 2014). The reality of professional practice is that it occurs in organizations and communities among groups and teams who have to collaborate, solve problems, learn together, balance conflicting priorities, innovate ideas and solutions, resolve conflict, and respond to churning change. Providing CPE that offers an update in knowledge to comply with regulations with little regard for the systems where practice occurs lacks innovation or acknowledgement about the dynamics of professional practice. It is probably more accurate to view it as "professional education" not "*continuing* professional education."

Individualism Versus Community of Practice Orientation. Increased regulation of professional practice and the tendency toward the update model of CPE puts the burden on individual practitioners to maintain and update their CPE, often to comply with association mandates. Yet, there is a lack of evidence-based CPE and a systemic approach that ensures its quality and completeness (Brockett & Bauer, 1998). The update model tends to separate the individual from the system of professional practice and place the learning on isolated individuals. Yet, in reality, professionals do not practice by themselves and CPE is lacking in its development of communities of practice within professions where generative learning can occur.

Instrumentality Versus Generativity. Typical CPE treats professional practice as static and unevolving, focused more on repetition of instrumental and technical skills than proactively responding to the problems of its key stakeholders. This approach corresponds with CPE's narrow definition of professional knowledge termed *functionalist* rationality by Cervero (1988) where knowledge is objective and detached from the professionals who develop it and the contexts where they apply it. Instrumentalist approaches do not help professionals develop capacity to act in the moment—that is, to be generative in their practice by accurately assessing situations, individuals, social contexts, and taking mindful action in the midst of ambiguity and shifting practice. CPE is not as effective as it could be at developing individual and collective professional capacities to make decisions in practice. Instead, CPE regulates professionals and professional knowledge as a way of protecting the public from incompetent practice.

Relevance and Effectiveness. CPE must be relevant. Regardless of global investment in CPE, there is little evidence to show that it has tangibly affected practice or created good outcomes (Clark et al., 2015). CPE has been critiqued for focusing on compliance rather than competency (Cervero & Daley, 2011; Clyde, 1998; Queeney, 2000; Wilson & Cervero, 2014). Content objectivity might also be questionable when CPE providers have vested interests, such as pharma support of continuing medical education. Learning is sometimes overlooked entirely in the design, delivery, and assessment of CPE. A Malaysian study of nurses showed that they perceived CPE as important, even if they were not active participants and that they were most likely to attend when topics were relevant, especially advanced practice skills (Chong, Francis, Cooper & Abdullah, 2014).

Inadequate CPE. CPE literature overflows with consistent complaints that change is long overdue. Despite the laments that CPE is not working as effectively as it should be, the debate about CPE remains relatively unchanged: CPE is disconnected from practice, too instrumentalist, and short shrifts culture, context, and collaboration. If we hope to transcend these debates and resulting ineffective CPE, it is time to get serious about changing the language, practice, culture, and standards of CPE. Yet, how do we do that? The ambiguous, fluid, fragmented nature of life and work requires professionals to act nimbly, swiftly, and collectively. "To quickly adapt to change, today's workforce must be collaborative and conversational across departments, skill sets and geographies" (Cotter, 2015, p. 12).

CPE for T-Shaped Professionals

One strategy to help professionals be more adaptive in ambiguous, changing context is to reevaluate their preparation and training. An alternative conceptualization of professional learning and development can be found in the "T-shaped professional"—a metaphor for workers possessing both depth and breadth of skills and knowledge (Cotter, 2015; Harris, 2009). To visualize the "T-shaped professional," imagine the vertical line of a "T" (Figure 5.1), representing a specific area of deep professional, disciplinary, and systems knowledge such as medicine along with a broader understanding (the horizontal line of the "T") of relational and cognitive skills that doctors connect to their deep knowledge such as emotional intelligence, empathy, presence, and communication skills. T-shaped professionals possess a repertoire of skills supporting collaboration and innovation with the other individuals and groups in their system (e.g., nurses and pharmacists) in contrast to the more siloed way in which CPE assumes professionals to operate with a bias toward updating their current knowledge in isolation.

Figure 5.1. T-Shaped Professional

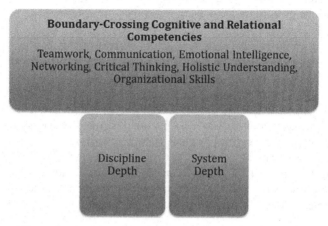

Source: Adapted from Cotter (2015) and Harris (2009).

T-shaped professionals "are deep problem solvers in their home discipline but also capable of interacting with and understanding specialists from a wide range of disciplines and functional areas" (Ing, 2008, n.p.). They have specialized knowledge and expertise along with the ability to broaden thinking and collaboration across disciplines and settings. They also keenly understand business, technology, people, and culture, and draw on insight and experience in ways that promote action and innovation within the organization (Harris, 2009).

Given CPE's challenges, I propose a new conceptual framework based on the T-shaped professional. I have adapted the framework illustrated in Figure 5.2. T-shaped CPE incorporates disciplinary and system depth (the vertical part of the T) with key boundary-crossing competencies crucial to developing as a collaborative, communicative, multidisciplinary professional (the horizontal part of the T). The next sections develop the idea of "T-shaped CPE."

T-Shaped CPE: Discipline Depth (Vertical Part of the "T"). Professionals engage in specialized training with expectations of developing into discipline experts . Discipline depth includes not only highly developed expertise based on the best evidence but also ethical practice. Udani and Udani (2012) proposed an integral framework for CPE that incorporates ethical development of professionals. They made several observations about CPE including that it is enduring and actively pursued by individuals based on their goals and initiative and a common good among members of a profession. They recommended that professional associations assume a more active and direct role in advocating ethical education as a part of CPE. I have taken the traditional trajectory of expertise development and used it to define professional

Figure 5.2. T-Shaped CPE

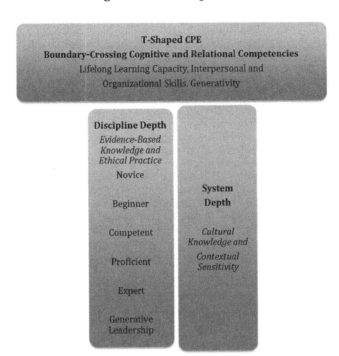

discipline depth and added a new category based on the need to transcend expert knowledge by being a generative leader and learner. Table 5.1 summarizes these developmental stages.

Building expertise is a starting point for many professionals once they complete their education. Yet, Yorks and Nicolaides (2013) posited that expertise has limitations because it may prevent professionals from being generative by causing overreliance on disciplinary knowledge while ignoring the social context. Generative professionals tune into their learning, reflect on practice, and develop provocative insights in the process. Yorks and Nicolaides identified the "expert-achiever mindset" (p. 9) or how learners learn powerfully from experience and simultaneously become better learners. This type of learning is system embedded—the learning comes from experience in the system, not as a by-product of acting on the system. This is why deep knowledge must include both discipline and system depth. The goal is for learners to consider innovative options, improvise, seek new insight, and not follow rule-bound paths on which they have built their expertise. Generativity helps professionals be more effective learners in times and contexts characterized by uncertainty and ambiguity.

T-Shaped CPE: System Depth (Vertical Part of the "T"). Disciplinary depth is necessary but not sufficient in high-performing professions.

Table 5.1. Professional Knowing Based on Development Stage

Novice	Shows minimal or textbook knowledge of the discipline and needs close supervision. Demonstrates little understanding of complexity or big picture comprehension of the discipline.
Beginner	Displays a working knowledge of key aspects of practice and accomplishes straightforward tasks with supervision.
Competent	Possesses a solid background and experiential knowledge. Uses judgment, planning, and analysis to cope with complex situations.
Proficient	Demonstrates depth of understanding of practice/discipline and takes a holistic approach to the profession and performs efficiently and effectively. Takes full responsibility for work (and perhaps others) and is confident in decision making.
Expert	Possesses authoritative knowledge and deep tacit understanding of the discipline. Sees the overall big picture and has a holistic grasp of the field. Demonstrates mastery and the ability for visionary thinking beyond conventional standards and practices of the profession. Mentors and teaches others in the discipline.
Generative Leader and Learner	Demonstrates expertise plus the ability to adapt to ambiguous and unpredictable social contexts and situations in the moment and take mindful action. Engages in continual reflection in and on experience, learns from it, and teaches others.

Source: Adapted from Benner (1984).

As professionals build expertise, they must simultaneously understand the system where the profession resides. This helps professionals practice more generative leadership and learning. For example, an accountant must have deep disciplinary knowledge about numbers, finances, and taxes. Accountants must also understand various systems to accomplish their profession such as the financial system and tax law within their particular state and nation while working alongside other accountants, clients, organizations, and other nations to accomplish their work. They also have to respond to financial crises and volatile markets. System depth means understanding the culture of the profession and organization, as well as the social context and dynamics where the profession plays out in practice. This knowledge equips professionals to respond more nimbly and creatively to unpredictable problems and uncertain contexts. Yorks and Nicolaides (2013) viewed complex adaptive systems as things that require framing so learners can understand how they are learning within various contexts that have varying degrees of uncertainty and ambiguity (profession, life, community, etc.) and from the experiences they have in them. This includes having cultural knowledge and contextual sensitivity.

Cultural Knowledge. Just like various groups in society, professions have rules, rites, and rituals that shape members' beliefs, values, and behaviors combining to form professional culture. Culture is a set of basic assumptions that social groups invent, discover, or develop as a means of coping with problems and adapting to the external context (Schein, 1991). Culture gets passed down from old members who teach new members. Culture is often described as encompassing three levels: basic underlying assumptions, espoused beliefs and values, and artifacts.

Positive culture plays an important role in reinforcing CPE (Clark et al., 2015). Elements of a positive culture include strategic institutional commitment to CPE that supports the attainment of individual and organizational goals. CPE should also be planned in accord with organizational strategy, rather than arbitrarily. This works best if all stakeholders readily communicate and collaborate. There also needs to be instructional support for the application of new learning in to practice through mentoring or coaching. T-shaped professionals are able to communicate across social, economic, and cultural boundaries to innovate, collaborate, strengthen their profession, and advance professional knowledge. They also have the capacity to reflect on cultural assumptions, challenge, and potentially change them in collaboration with colleagues.

Clark, Draper, and Rogers (2015) identified ways to enhance the impact of CPE on practice across the stages of design, delivery and evaluation. They emphasized that a focus on evaluating outcomes of CPE has caused the neglect of underlying processes of positive organizational culture, effective stakeholder partnerships, and a supportive learning environment that are essential to effective CPE.

Contextual Sensitivity. In addition to cultural awareness that contributes to system knowledge, professionals need to be sensitive to the context of their work. Merriam and Bierema (2014) defined context as understanding how globalization, the information society, technology, and changing demographics affect living and learning. This includes managing the fluidity and ambiguity characteristic of contemporary life in collaboration with groups and teams. Professionals need to be aware of how the broader context affects the profession and develop savvy for dealing with it and the clashing values and goals that characterize diverse communities. Yet, the socially embedded nature of learning is ignored in the current configuration of CPE.

Gorman (2003) advocated that CPE should incorporate personal development and contextual awareness. Context is important because professionals make decisions in many cases where no single best solution exists and they need the ability to assess risks as part of their expert knowledge. Eraut (1994) identified five types of knowledge that are relevant in work context: acquiring information or assessing the situation, skilled behavior or ability to manage situations, deliberative processes such as decision making, giving information, and meta-processes for directing and controlling one's own behavior or self-management. Gorman (2003) suggests that within context, "'knowing how' is as important as 'knowing what'" (p. 248). Skill is also important and encompasses the person performing the skill, the social estimation of the skill involved, plus the task itself (Ainley, 1993). Complex professional contexts create confusion and uncertainty while also provide opportunities for understanding professional practice in new ways and how social, economic, political and cultural transformations create new possibilities (Yorks & Nicolaides, 2013).

T-Shaped CPE: Boundary-Crossing Cognitive and Relational Competencies (Horizontal Part of the "T"). The T-shaped professional's development of disciplinary expertise and system depth is insufficient to be a fully functioning professional without developing capacity for interdisciplinary dialogue and collaboration. This allows professionals to engage in problem solving using their expertise and system insight in collaboration with a range of professionals from other disciplines (Ing, 2008). I propose that the breadth of skills for professionals includes lifelong learning capacity, interpersonal and organizational skills, and generative leadership. There are likely others specific to particular professions.

Lifelong Learning Capacity. Lifelong learning is the capacity for critical thinking, problem solving, transferring new knowledge to work context, and ongoing growth and commitment to professional learning across the life span. It is a skill that spans disciplines and systems and important for professionals to cultivate continuously. Because CPE is the lifelong process of systematically maintaining and improving knowledge, competence, and skills among professionals, it is aligned with broader life learning as a means of enhancing learning and development and acting for the public good.

CPE embraced lifelong learning when it began considering the processes of adult and continuing education as well as human resource development (Cervero, 1988). A key process of lifelong learning is informal learning— the learning that occurs as we engage in work and life through observation, conversation, mistake detection and correction, teaching others, and so forth. Lifelong learning helps professionals' skill refinement, identity development, the formation of moral and ethical standards, role modeling, and passing along professional skills to others. Yet, CPE has done a poor job helping professionals become better informal learners through sharpening their skills of reflection and capacity for learning both in and from experience.

Change and learning go hand in hand, and thus an important aspect of lifelong learning is the capacity to transform thought and action as a result of learning. Also known as transformative learning, this process promotes changes in individual thought and practice that have the potential to reconceptualize practice. Yorks and Nicolaides (2013) advocated that educators should help adults build capacity to make sense of the demands placed on them within complex contexts that move from dependence to independence to interdependence, with the assumption that professionals recognize how they are in relationship to others and their learning in complex contexts.

Interpersonal and Organizational Skills. Professionals do not work in a vacuum. Professional life involves engagement with clients, employees, colleagues, associations, and other professionals. Being a professional requires collaboration, problem solving, networking, negotiating, educating, and decision making in ambiguous, unpredictable, shifting context. All of these activities are done with other individuals and teams. Effective interpersonal skill requires emotional intelligence, effective communication, appreciation for diversity and inclusion, empathy, and timeliness.

Helping professionals develop interpersonal skills will serve them throughout their career. Particularly important is developing professions that are sensitive to issues of equity and inclusion. Yet, Ross-Gordon and Brooks (2004) lamented that CPE has not developed an integrated vision for creating more inclusive environments within professions. Ways CPE can better address diversity and inclusion would be to actively advocate for equity, diversity, and inclusion both in CPE and in the professions. "For adult educators whose mission is to engage and reenvision democratic action, to develop deliberate learning pathways that enhance adults' participation in society, and to provide intentional space for inclusion and diversity that grow adults' capacities to meet the demands of this complex liquid modernity, *generative learning within ambiguity* provides a shelter for adults to shape new mutual realties" (Nicolaides, 2015, p. 16).

Professionals also need to develop organizational skills. These include the ability to see the big picture, focus on details, plan and oversee projects, solve problems, prioritize goals, supervise staff, schedule tasks, organize resources, budget, manage time effectively, and meet deadlines. Organizational skills also determine how well professionals respond to both planned and unplanned change.

Generativity. The state of generativity is one of consciousness. It is the ability to look beyond oneself and the profession to collaborate with and serve others in ways that promote holistic social action. It is a state of openness to taking mindful, ethical action and making change at the individual, profession, organization, and system level. The outcome is the sustainability, relevance, and timeliness of the professional and profession.

Generative learning and leadership positions professionals to learn and enhance the boundary-crossing aspects of the T-shaped professional. Yorks and Nicolaides (2013) contrasted adaptive and generative learning. Adaptive learning is how learners cope with changes in professional context or adjust to existing practices, policies, regulations, products, or services—essentially the focus of CPE. Generative learning is how professionals create new approaches that disrupt professional practice with innovative change to respond to ambiguous and unpredictable contexts. They observed, "By an enhanced *capacity for engaging in generative learning through inquiry,* we mean having *an immediate awareness of how one is in relationship with ambiguity and uncertain challenges of one's environment while maintaining and continually testing one's actions with one's intentionality*" (Yorks & Nicolaides, 2013, pp. 4–5). Generative learning helps professionals question assumptions, change thought or action, and more effectively confront disruptive environments where their prevailing assumptions no longer work (Chiva, Grandio, & Alegre, 2010).

Generative CPE

Professional excellence depends on new forms of learning and leading. With the recent market crashes and financial reporting fiascoes, Frecka and Reckers (2010) suggested that it is time for national dialogue about changing societal needs and the adequacy of professional training provided in accounting. Their advice applies to all professions. They advocated for more active stakeholder assessment in the quality and level of satisfaction with professional development. Current training has allowed a gap to widen between education and practice. They call for rethinking accounting professional education in ways that are relevant for all professions and aligned with the T-shaped professional:

- Foreground values of quality, integrity, transparency, and accountability
- Advocate for transformational changes in curricula including:
  - What it means to be a "professional"
  - Higher level interpersonal and communication skills
  - Advanced problem solving for complex environments where best answers are evasive
- Broaden initial training to cover the context and environment of the profession
- Bridge academic and professional educational stakeholders
- Emphasize continuous individual and collaborative learning

The current context is churning with change and expectations for social responsibility are prominent. What role can CPE play in creating and enabling healthy organizations and sustainable, socially responsible professions that integrate ethical and moral responsibility? Yorks and Nicolaides (2013) argued that there is an educational need to develop pedagogy appropriate for addressing the complex contexts adults face in their professional and personal lives. Yet, they observed that course designs intended to prepare adults are lacking as they tend to provide rigid application of ready-made solutions that do not work for adults who need to be better prepared to take mindful action on challenges that are embedded in ambiguity and uncertainty. They called for creating professional education that allows adults to expand their capacity to make meaning, and take timely action under conditions of uncertainty and ambiguity that are appropriate to their complex contexts.

Educative design, according to Yorks and Nicolaides (2013) should prepare learners to learn through complex challenges characterized by uncertainty and ambiguity of a personal, vocational, or civic nature. They suggest that educative designs that accomplish these results incorporate:

Inquiry in action: Using activities such as action learning, action research, or action science engages professionals in focusing on ambiguous challenges they confront in professional practice.

Reflexive meaning making: Using inquiry groups to promote dialogue focused on making sense of professional dilemmas and experience. This helps professionals build awareness of the assumptions they have developed over years of experience and gives them a basis for reframing thought and action.

Timely action: Learners use action inquiry and reflexivity to take effective, timely action while remaining open to the unexpected surprises that emerge in practice.

Course design to help learners take more mindful action when their world is embedded in uncertainty and ambiguity cannot be left to the rigid application of ready-made solutions or learning activities, such as traditional reading, lecture, and restructured classroom activities (Yorks & Nicolaides, 2013). Instead, course designs should give learners self-directed opportunities to explore how they learn within action in social context and with others.

CPE has languished with failure to be innovative, context based, relevant, or generative. It is time to rethink how we are preparing professionals for work and contributing to their field and society. The T-shaped professional framework holds promise for creating and sustaining more holistic, impactful CPE to help professionals more fluidly navigate the professional white water they encounter on a daily basis.

References

Ainley, P. (1993). *Class and skill: Changing divisions of knowledge and labour*. New York: Cassell.

Balan, D. (2005). *Contextual factors associated with continuing professional education practices of selected professional providers in Malaysia* (Unpublished doctoral dissertation). Universiti Putra Malaysia, Serdang, Selangor, Malaysia.

Benner, P. (1984). *From novice to expert: Excellence and power in clinical nursing practice*. Menlo Park, NJ: Prentice Hall.

Bierema, L. L., & Eraut, M. (2004). Workplace-focused learning: Perspective on continuing professional education and human resource development. *Advances in Developing Human Resources*, 6(10), 52–68.

Brockett, M., & Bauer, M. (1998). Continuing professional education: Responsibilities and possibilities. *Journal of Continuing Education in the Health Professions*, 18, 235–243.

Cervero, R. M. (1988). *Effective continuing education for the professions*. San Francisco, CA: Jossey-Bass.

Cervero R. M., & Daley, B. J. (2011). Continuing professional education: Multiple stakeholders and agendas. In K. Rubenson (Ed.), *Adult learning and education* (pp. 140–145). Oxford, UK: Elsevier.

Chiva, R., Grandio, A., & Alegre, J. (2010). Adaptive and generative learning: Implications from complexity theories. *International Journal of Management Reviews*, 12(2), 114–129.

Chong, M. C., Francis, K., Cooper, S., & Abdullah, K. L. (2014). Current continuing professional education practice among Malaysian nurses. *Nursing Research and Practice*, 2014, 1–6.

Clark, E., Draper, J., & Rogers, J. (2015). Illuminating the process: Enhancing the impact of continuing professional education on practice: A literature review. *Nurse Education Today*, 35, 388–394.

Clyde, N. J. (1998). CPE is broke: Let's fix it. *Journal of Accountancy, 186*(6), 77–83.

Cotter, P. (2015). Hiring and development, down to a T. *Chief Learning Officer, 14*(2), 12.

Cotterill-Walker, S. M. (2012). Where is the evidence that master's level nursing education makes a difference in patient care? *Nurse Education Today, 32*(1), 57–64.

Dirkx, J., Gilley, J. W., & Gilley, A. M. (2004). Change theory in CPE and HRD: Toward a holistic view of learning and change in work. *Advances in Developing Human Resources, 6*(1), 35–51.

Eraut, M. (1985). Knowledge creation and knowledge use in professional contexts. *Studies in Higher Education, 10*(2), 117–133.

Eraut, M. (1994). Developing professional knowledge and competence. London: Falmer Press.

Frecka, T. J., & Reckers, P. M. J. (2010). Rekindling the debate: What's right and what's wrong with masters of accountancy programs: The staff auditor's perspective. *Issues in Accounting Education, 25*(2), 215–226.

Goodall, J., Day, C., Lindsay, G., Muijs, D., & Harris, A. (2005). *Evaluating the impact of continuing professional development* (Research Report No. 659). London: Department of Education and Skills.

Gorman, H. (2003). Which skills do care managers need? A research project on skills, competency, and continuing professional development. *Social Work Education, 22*(2), 245–259.

Grant, J. (2011). *The good CPD guide: A practical guide to managed continuing professional development in medicine* (2nd ed.). Milton Keynes, UK: The Open University Centre for Education in Medicine.

Harris, P. (2009). Help wanted: "T-shaped" skills to meet 21st century needs. *T+D, 63*(9), 42–47.

Houle, C. (1980). *Continuing education in the professions.* San Francisco, CA: Jossey-Bass.

Ing, D. (2008, September 6). T-shaped professionals, t-shaped skills, hybrid managers. *Coevolving innovations.* Retrieved from http://coevolving.com/blogs/index.php/archive/t-shaped-professionals-t-shaped-skills-hybrid-managers/

Jeris, L. H. (2010). Continuing professional education. In C. E. Kasworm, A. D. Rose, & J. M. Ross-Gordon (Eds.), *Handbook of adult and continuing education* (pp. 275–282). Thousand Oaks, CA: Sage.

Jeris, L. H., & Conway, A. E. (2003). Time to regrade the terrain of continuing professional education: Views from practitioners. *Adult Learning, 14*(1), 34–36. doi: 10.1177/104515950301400110

Jeris, L. H., & Daley, B. (2004). Orienteering for boundary spanning: Reflections on the journey to date and suggestions for moving forward. *Advances in developing human resources, 6*(1), 101–115. doi:10.1177/1523422303260420

Kegan, R. (1995). *In over our heads: The mental demands of modern life.* Cambridge: Harvard University Press.

Lahti, M., Kontio, R., Pitkanen, A., & Valimaki, M. (2014). Knowledge transfer from an e-learning course to clinical practice. *Nurse Education Today, 34*(5), 842–847.

Merriam, S. B., & Bierema, L. L. (2014). *Adult learning: Linking theory and practice.* San Francisco, CA: Jossey-Bass.

Nicolaides, A. (2015). Generative learning: Adults learning within ambiguity. *Adult Education Quarterly, 65,* 1–17.

Nowlen, P. M. (1988). *A new approach to continuing education for business and the professions: The performance model.* Old Tappan, NJ: Macmillan.

Queeney, D. S. (2000). Continuing professional education. In A. Wilson & E. Hayes (Eds.), *Handbook of adult & continuing education* (pp. 375–392). San Francisco, CA: Jossey-Bass.

Ross-Gordon, J., & Brooks, A. K. (2004). Diversity in human resource development and continuing professional education: What does it mean for the workforce, clients, and professionals? *Advances in Developing Human Resources, 6*(1), 69–85.

Schein, E. H. (1991). *Organizational culture and leadership: A dynamic view.* San Francisco, CA: Jossey-Bass.

Sleezer, C. M., Conti, G. J., & Nolan, R. E. (2004). Comparing CPE and HRD programs: Definitions, theoretical foundations, outcomes, and measures of quality. *Advances in Developing Human Resources, 6*(1), 20–34.

Udani, Z. A. S., & Udani D. S. (2012). Exploring an integral framework on continuing professional education. *Euro Asia Journal of Management, 22*(1–2), 101–116.

Vaill, P. B. (1996). *Learning as a way of being: Strategies for survival in a world of permanent white water.* San Francisco, CA: Jossey-Bass.

Van Loo, J. B., & Rocco, T. S. (2006). Differentiating CPE from training: Reconsidering terms, boundaries and economic factors. *Human Resource Development Review, 5*(2), 202–227.

Wessels, S. B. (2007). Accountants' perceptions of the effectiveness of mandatory continuing professional education. *Accounting Education: An International Journal, 16*(4), 365–378.

Wilson, A., & Cervero, R. (2014). Continuing professional education in the United States: A strategic analysis of current and future directions. In B. Käpplinger & S. Robak (Eds.), *Changing configurations in adult education in transitional times: International perspectives in different countries* (pp. 211–222). New York, NY: Peter Lang.

Yorks, L., & Nicolaides, A. (2013). Toward and integral approach for evolving mindsets for generative learning and timely action in the midst of ambiguity. *Teachers College Record, 115,* 1–26.

LAURA L. BIEREMA *is professor and associate dean for academic programs in the College of Education at the University of Georgia.*

6

This chapter focuses on how to negotiate power and interest among multiple stakeholders to develop continuing professional education programs as graduate study for those in the health and medical professions.

Developing Continuing Professional Education in the Health and Medical Professions Through Collaboration

Elizabeth J. Tisdell, Margaret Wojnar, Elizabeth Sinz

Continuing professional education (CPE) happens in many forms and contexts. It often happens through programs that offer continuing education units (CEUs) to specific occupation groups (Coady, 2015; Jeris, 2010) and many healthcare professionals are required to participate to maintain their licensure or certification. Other development activities for professionals may arise through professional collaborations based on common interests and specific needs. The purpose of this chapter is to discuss the formation of a CPE program in the health and medical professions though graduate coursework in adult education at Penn State University that developed out of relationships with colleagues at Penn State College of Medicine. We write as colleagues, one of us as an adult education professor and coordinator of the program (Tisdell), the other two as physician educators on the faculty (Wojnar and Sinz) at the College of Medicine who have been participants in the graduate program as CPE. Our focus is on how the program developed in response to a specific need identified through collaborative dialogue and what was taught, learned, and applied based on our ever-expanding knowledge of each other's contexts and needs. Given our different roles, we speak here in different voices. First, Libby Tisdell outlines how the program developed and its theoretical underpinnings; then as participants in the program, Peg Wojnar and Lisa Sinz provide examples of what was learned and applied in their healthcare education practice.

Theoretical Orientations: Negotiating Power and Interest (Elizabeth "Libby" Tisdell)

Developing adult education programs of any type, including CPE, is always about identifying needs and negotiating power and interest among multiple stakeholders (Cervero & Wilson, 2006). Nearly 10 years ago, a colleague at

New Directions for Adult and Continuing Education, no. 151, Fall 2016 © 2016 Wiley Periodicals, Inc.
Published online in Wiley Online Library (wileyonlinelibrary.com) • DOI: 10.1002/ace.20196

the College of Medicine approached the adult education faculty at Penn State Harrisburg (primarily my colleague Dr. Ed Taylor and me) about consulting on a CPE program to foster appropriate teaching methodologies in clinical education, based on adult learning theories. In the next 5 years, we worked together on a number of small projects out of shared interests that had mutual benefits. Many collaborative relationships developed that were part of the networking necessary to develop a larger scale CPE program for clinical educators and to put it in place. Over time, we developed a four-course (12-credit) Graduate Certificate in Adult Education in the Health and Medical Professions, with the agreement that once completed, learners could transfer the coursework into a master's or doctoral program (in adult education) if they met the degree admission criteria. The first course was taught in the fall of 2011; participants have been physicians, veterinarians, nurses, respiratory therapists, physicians' assistants, nurse practitioners, faculty teaching in science and research, and some who work in administrative capacities. About three fourths of those who complete the graduate certificate continue into the master's or doctoral programs in adult education. Because physicians already have a professional doctorate (an MD) they usually opt to complete the master's program; this is the case for two coauthors of this paper (Wojnar and Sinz). Others who continue do so in the degree program that meets their overall goals.

Program Development. Program development typically begins with a needs assessment (Caffarella & Daffron, 2013). In this case, it was the College of Medicine that identified the need for development of clinical physician educators and solicited our expertise. As initial players in the conversation, we were simply discussing the relevance of adult learning theory to clinical teaching. The certificate program as CPE developed over time among those who wanted to engage with colleagues with similar interests in teaching and learning in a community of practice (Wenger, 2000). It also expanded beyond physician educators, because those who work and educate in health care do so in an interprofessional context. Hence, the focus of our CPE program was ultimately geared to interprofessional education in the health and medical professions.

In developing CPE programs, having buy-in from someone in a leadership position from the particular profession is key to program development. In this case, the person who initially contacted us facilitating entry into conversations about adult learning theory as applied to an area of practice for medical faculty development became an associate dean. Hence, she knew how to negotiate the system in the College of Medicine. Our collaboration as adult education faculty members with tenure provided enough social capital and know-how on our end to navigate the politics of graduate education. Hence, having champions and collaborators with enough institutional power and a good collaborative relationship with mutual benefits to both sides was key to making the program happen as a form of CPE.

Learning to understand the discourse of the applied practice field is also crucial for developing a beneficial program for its intended participants. The

CPE program is in adult education in the health and medical professions and is intended for a wide variety of clinician–educators. As such, we recognized that in order to be responsive to their learning needs, we needed to understand what health and medical professionals do in their clinical teaching. In regard to learning what physician educators do, adult education faculty colleagues collaboratively conducted a study with a physician at the medical school examining teaching beliefs and practices of medical educators (Taylor, Tisdell, & Gusic, 2007). Adult education faculty also shadowed physicians doing clinical rounds; we were impressed by their knowledge and skill in patient care and their teaching people at the bedside who are at very different stages of knowledge and development—from medical students, to interns, to residents, who are also learning from nurses, respiratory therapists, and social workers.

From this study of their context, we learned the everyday discourse of teaching in the clinical setting is focused more on the practicalities of teaching a differential diagnosis, appropriate patient care, a focus on teaching and learning though example, role modeling, scaffolding, and mentorship as one becomes more proficient over time. The everyday teaching discourse tends not to focus as much on examining one's underlying assumptions about what counts as knowledge and other such epistemological questions that are part of adult education discourse. Hence in developing the CPE program, we learned the practical discourse in health/medical education, at the same time that we began introducing learners to adult education discourse that explores philosophy, learning theory, and how knowledge is constructed, not only through clinical trials of large randomized samples but also by how people negotiate power and interest.

Curriculum Development. Part of the discourse in CPE for the medical and health professions is around curriculum development from a traditional perspective employing a six-step approach that focuses on identifying the problem, doing a needs assessment, establishing goals and objectives, educational strategies, implementing all of the above, and doing an assessment (Kern, Thomas, & Hughes, 2009). Evidence-based medicine (EBM) is heavily emphasized, which is the context of most ongoing CPE in the health and medical professions. There is little discussion of how one's underlying philosophy of education informs teaching and minimal emphasis on the examination of how power relations shape decisions about curriculum development or program planning in the way Cervero and Wilson (2006) discuss as an iterative process of negotiating power and interest. There is, however, discussion of the "hidden curriculum" (Lemp & Seale, 2004), which is about what gets "taught" in covert ways about how clinical work gets done but isn't spoken about directly, which can indeed be related to power and interest.

The point here is that in developing the program and curriculum, adult education faculty needed to learn to listen to and learn from the discourse in the health and medical professions. With this in mind, as we developed the curriculum, we focused on bridging the content areas of adult education with health and medical professions education as CPE that could be applied

Figure 6.1. Negotiating Power and Interest for Curriculum Development in the Health and Medical Professions

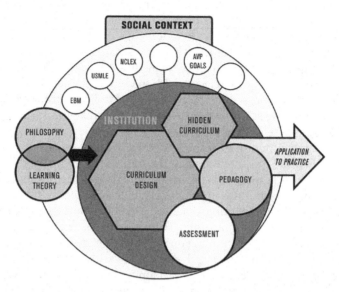

directly to participants' teaching practice. We developed and used the graphic in Figure 6.1, building on the work of Cervero and Wilson (2006), which visually depicts the processes by which power and interests for curriculum development might be negotiated. We used the graphic both to design our own curriculum and to help learners think about curriculum development in their own teaching context. Although the graphic is for curriculum design in the health and medical professions, it would be applicable to curriculum design in most settings.

In this graphic, we begin by considering the social context of practice and how one's beliefs and assumptions as philosophy along with how learning theory inform curriculum design in this particular institutional context. We ask participants to consider all the stakeholders and power issues they need to consider that affect what curricular and pedagogical decisions they make and to depict these in the small circles. Some of these related to the health and medical professions include the push of evidence-based medicine (EBM), guidelines from oversight organizations like the Association of American Medical Colleges (AAMC) as typically overseen by academic vice presidents (AVPs) for what's needed for programs to maintain certification in various accreditation bodies, what people need to know to pass board exams such as the U.S. Medical Licensing Exam (USMLE) or the Nursing Certification Licensing Exam (NCLEX), and what students and other faculty deem as "good teaching" that will affect learners and the patients that they ultimately serve. The open circles on the figure indicate other things that may affect how curriculum is negotiated at the particular institution. Although curriculum design issues are largely about what is included for content, it is also about thinking about what is being taught through the "hidden curriculum," deciding on what pedagogy or strategies for teaching and what assessment measures will be used to determine effectiveness. Finally, there is an emphasis on how to apply it to practice not only with learners but also for the benefit of the patients whom they serve.

As in any graduate program, there is also an emphasis on writing papers at the graduate level. But we emphasize trying to write for eventual publication and doing projects that directly relate to practice. How learners spin their analysis and apply their learning about these issues depends on the learner and the specialization area. The following discussion by two coauthors and senior faculty members and physicians from the College of Medicine in different areas of practice provides some example.

Working with an Interprofessional Team in Intensive Care (Margaret Wojnar, MD)

I am an intensive care physician, trained to care for patients in the intensive care unit (ICU). I currently work in an academic medical center where as a medical educator I instruct nurses, medical students, residents, and fellows interested in critical care medicine. I had no formal instruction in adult education until recently through the graduate certificate and then the master's program discussed previously. This is a CPE program that has helped me collaborate with other professionals to solve practical education-related problems in the ICU. One such problem is discussed here.

Background and Context as a Medical Educator. As a person who has attended many professional development sessions on teaching and assessment, I learned many strategies but still struggled with how best to educate my students. The changes in Accreditation Council for Graduate Medical Education (ACGME) work hours for residents, the complexity of patient cases in the ICU due to advances in medical care, and pressure from medical administration to be more efficient and cost effective with patient care heightened this struggle. Such changes meant the time I have to teach needs to be integrated with the time for residents and other learners as I care for patients. My many attempts at using different strategies to educate my learners were often derailed due to time constraints or a clinical crisis that interrupted a session. Clearly, I needed a different approach because the education I provided seemed fractured and uneven.

Participating in the Graduate Certificate and Master's Program

When an opportunity to learn about adult education at my institution became available, I eagerly joined. My first class with the adult education faculty was transformational as I quickly learned that how I was taught had influenced my frame and was part of the reason I was frustrated with my educational sessions. With the first class, I felt both illiterate and frustrated with new language, as well as exhilarated and challenged. But I persisted and soon began to understand the influence of different kinds of authority on me and how it was affecting what I did with my learners.

Theories of learning, power, and interest were discussed as part of my graduate-level coursework in adult education. Examining my own philosophy of education and how that shaped how I taught was enlightening, as I understood more about adult education. I realized that learning opportunities exist everywhere and that the ICU was a living classroom. I learned about the range of factors that influenced my students, how emotions affect what they learn, and the importance of reflection and debriefing. I appreciated that my patients and their families hold perspectives on things, too, and that it was important to hear and to learn from them. My perspective and the lenses through which I evaluated experiences changed. I better understood privilege and the power and the responsibility that came with being an adult educator and my role as teacher/educator in my particular context. This sparked within me the beginning of a large interprofessional learning project that I employed as part of my coursework.

Application to Interprofessional Practice. While working in the ICU, my social worker and care coordinator approached me about several resident-led meetings that occurred with different families and expressed concern that the residents did not conduct these meeting very well. They noticed that the residents' meeting skills were uneven or lacking and wondered whether there was a better way to train residents in conducting a family meeting; they were willing to work with me to solve this problem. Family meetings are an important gathering of key family members and patient care providers, such as the physician, nurse, or social worker or care coordinator. The physician's usual responsibility is to lead the meeting and act as a content expert for medical information. Whoever leads the meeting sets the tone of the discussion, making this a key role. In my working area, there had been no specific training for family meetings. The resident, as a learner, would first observe several proceedings and then would be expected to lead a meeting. From the comments from my staff, this method was insufficient.

As part of my own CPE in the graduate coursework in adult education, I was encouraged to take educational problems or needs from my workplace and use/apply my learning from the classwork to solve practice problems and to build solutions. As there was no educational program for resident education around family meetings, a plan was needed. With information gleaned from my classes, literature searches, and collaboration of interprofessional groups within the institution, including the palliative care service and the ICU social worker and care coordinator, a blueprint for family meetings was designed and a basic curriculum outlined. From this, a family meeting booklet was drafted for use by anyone who was interested in learning the basic steps in running a family meeting. This approach was purposeful as roles for leading family meetings were changing. The physician was not always the leader of the meeting as they were not always available, tied up with other patient care issues. Social workers, care coordinators, nurse practitioners, physician assistants, pastoral care providers, and medicine residents needed to know how to lead a family meeting. The importance of interprofessional teams to work collaboratively for patients cannot be overstated. Knowing how to perform family meetings well is crucial for quality patient care.

Continuing Effects. From our work on the family meeting format, the institution formed a working group to focus on the performance of family meetings, using the booklet as a guide. The institutional purpose was to meet a performance metric set by an insurer/third-party payer. There were secondary gains for this effort including the development of an electronic medical record family meeting note. This was used for primary data collection for the project but could also be used for future research. Another gain was the attention the institution was placing on the importance of family meetings. This attention enabled a shift in the culture of practice in the ICU whereby it is now expected that family meetings occur for each family versus an older view of holding a family meeting primarily for end-of-life discussions or critical choices in care. This culture shift in communication will ultimately improve the quality of care for patients and their families.

My journey into learning more about adult education has been very fulfilling, enabling, yet challenging. I have a better understanding of my role, my own philosophy, where I fit with regards to power and "truth" and the tensions that exist between the different elements, and how to negotiate power and interest for the educational benefits of our interprofessional team, and for the care of patients and their families. It has been a demanding excursion but one that has enriched all who have participated with me. Part of what I learned in the program is best summarized by Mandela (2003): "Education is the most powerful weapon which you can use to change the world."

Negotiating Power and Interest for Simulation Education (Elizabeth Sinz, MD, FCCM)

When I entered the certificate and ultimately the master's program discussed previously as CPE in the first cohort of students, I had already been an educator in anesthesiology and intensive care medicine and active in promoting simulation-based healthcare education for over a decade. Simulation allows opportunities for situated learning in a setting remote from actual practice (Gaba, 1992). In health care, this means that key aspects of clinical encounters are recreated so students can practice the skills, problem solving, and teamwork needed for real patient care in a safe and controlled learning environment that is similar to an actual clinical environment. As associate dean for clinical simulation for the Penn State University College of Medicine, I had designed the new simulation center, participated in local faculty development activities, and taken CPE courses through professional societies. I was a founder and past president of the international Society for Simulation in Healthcare, an academic multiprofessional society of simulation educators. I had led many workshops as an educator and developed with my interprofessional simulation team a 5-day "Teaching with Simulation" instructor course for healthcare educators from different professions and healthcare centers that had been offered yearly since 2008. As such, when I began this graduate program as CPE in 2011, I felt pretty confident in my teaching. Yet, that first course opened my eyes to how little I actually knew about educational theory and research beyond medicine.

Education, Power, and Responsibility. Although I had plowed through "the system" to move simulation-based education into the mainstream, none of my prior CPE courses had addressed the interplay among education, economics, and politics. Although I had lobbied for government and industry support of simulation educators and promoted the use of simulation for healthcare professionals (Sinz, 2007), I did not know anything about how educator activists like bell hooks (1994) and Paulo Freire (Horton & Freire, 1990) used emancipatory education to battle entrenched power for social change. Their stories inspired me to consider how I should strive to empower healthcare faculty to work together across professions to make clinical education more robust and safe. I realized my position as the director of an educational resource in a healthcare system gave me influence that could serve the entire faculty who wanted to change clinical teaching, which could shape the direction of healthcare education.

In the adult education graduate coursework as CPE, I learned there are many stakeholders involved in deciding what education is or should be. As a result of new thinking about negotiating power and interest, I reorganized the Penn State Hershey Clinical Simulation Center to build a stronger interprofessional support team and infrastructure for simulation faculty. This required many negotiations with administrators about money and outcomes, but I learned new ways to frame my requests and how to unite my goals with others in negotiating power and interest. This resulted in being able to hire an outstanding educator and manager with extensive simulation expertise and the consolidation of some of the disparate activities from other departments to create greater synergy within and among simulation support staff to better support clinical faculty. As a result, we have become a more effective interprofessional community of practice.

My team is engaged in research aimed at identifying the best ways to help people become excellent simulation instructors through course work, mentoring, and guidelines developed in our community of practice that relates both to our local educational efforts and those at the national level. This interchange between the local, and education in the larger healthcare world, is a way one can affect an entire education system. Hence, I continue to participate in national organizations with similar educational goals such as working with the American Heart Association to develop and publish their education

New Directions for Adult and Continuing Education • DOI: 10.1002/ace

guidelines. I also became an associate editor for the academic journal, *Simulation in Healthcare*, because broad-scale educational change happens by being involved in national or international professional organizations that affect educational policy. Thus, these graduate adult education courses as CPE have made me see myself as an activist educator, striving to bring about social and system-wide change in healthcare education while also advocating for education that improves care that affects my own patients. Both activities are part of the same goal.

Scholarship, Research, and Collaboration. One of the important things I have learned in my adult education graduate study was the importance of scholarship and new approaches to research—qualitative and action research in particular. In continuing to develop the 5-day experiential "Teaching with Simulation" course mentioned previously, we had essentially followed an action research process each year since 2008. We continually adapted and improved each iteration of the course and had saved and continued to use our extensive teacher notes and student comments, which functioned as "data." Recognizing that our insights and experience could help others, we performed a retrospective thematic analysis of our data over time and presented our research at the 2014 Adult Education Research Conference (Sinz, Rudy, Wojnar, & Bortner, 2014). My positivist background had never exposed me to the principles of qualitative approach, but I now recognize how profoundly this research can contribute to the improvement of practice and to scholarship.

Another important component of the graduate program in adult education as CPE was engagement in the classes themselves with faculty and students who were not involved in health care. Interacting with teachers from different backgrounds and disciplines exposed me to new ideas about the role of educators and made me think about ways we could collaborate as partners in adult education from a cross-disciplinary perspective that can relate to educational change on a larger scale. Out of these cross-collaborations, we developed a new graduate course in instructional and program design in medical education that includes components of simulation education as part of the course. Working on this article together is another example of collaborating across disciplines.

Initially, I anticipated this program would build my credibility and expose me to some new ideas, but I really did not anticipate just how much I would learn nor how much it would affect my work in simulation education and increase my interest and ability to collaborate across disciplines while drawing on the expertise of educators in non-healthcare fields and over time. The role all educators play is to increase the power of our learners. This CPE program changed my perspective about the role of an educator as an agent of change to a system and made me understand my own power. Now, I really see how the saying "knowledge is power" applies to me. To be sure, being part of this graduate program and what I have learned have been an extremely valuable part of my own CPE.

Conclusion

CPE happens in many settings and can happen quite effectively in graduate certificate or graduate degree programs in universities. But key to helping them be successful is being able to collaborate with colleagues across disciplines, as well as being able to negotiate power and interest among multiple stakeholders. But one of the many stakeholders and ultimately what we need to be concerned about in continuing education in the health and medical professions is how students and the patients they serve are going to be affected by that continuing education. In the stories we have told, we have considered what we have learned about negotiating power and interest, our own roles in it, and how we have collaborated and applied it in our practice in the service of learners and patients. There are many more stories to tell, but suffice it to say that being a part of the collaborative planning and delivery of a program as learners and teachers has been an important part of our own continuing professional education.

References

Caffarella, R., & Daffron, S. (2013). *Planning programs for adult learners*. San Francisco, CA: Jossey-Bass.

Cervero, R., & Wilson, A. (2006). *Working the planning table*. San Francisco, CA: Jossey-Bass.

Coady, M. (2015). From Houle to Dirkx: Continuing professional education (CPE), a critical-state-of-the-field. *Canadian Journal for the Study of Adult Education, 27*, 27–41.

Gaba, D. M. (1992). Improving anesthesiologists' performance by simulating reality. *Anesthesiology, 76*, 491–494.

hooks, b. (1994). *Teaching to transgress*. New York: Routledge.

Horton, M., & Freire, P. (1990). *We make the road by walking*. Philadelphia: Temple University Press.

Jeris, L. (2010). Continuing professional education. In C. Kasworm, A. Rose, & J. Ross-Gordon (Eds.), *2010 handbook of adult and continuing education*. Thousand Oaks, CA: Sage.

Kern, D., Thomas, P., & Hughes, M. (Eds.). (2009). *Curriculum development for medical education: A six-step approach*. Baltimore, MD: Johns Hopkins Press.

Lemp, H., & Seale, C. (2004). The hidden curriculum in undergraduate medical education: Qualitative study of medical students' perceptions of teaching. *British Medical Journal, 329*, 770–773.

Mandela, N. R. (2003, July 16). Presentation at the launch of Mindset Network. Retrieved from http://db.nelsonmandela.org/speeches/pub_view.asp?pg=item&ItemID=NMS909&txtstr=education%20is%20the%20most%20powerful

Sinz, E. (2007). 2006 simulation summit. *Simulation in Healthcare, 2*, 33–38.

Sinz, E., Rudy, S., Wojnar, M., & Bortner, T. (2014). Teaching simulation literacy in adult healthcare education: A qualitative action research study. In *Proceedings of the 55th Annual Adult Education Research Conference*. Middletown, PA: Penn State University.

Taylor, E., Tisdell, E., & Gusic, M. (2007). Teaching beliefs of medical educators: Perspectives on clinical teaching in pediatrics. *Medical Teacher, 29*, 371–376.

Wenger, E. (2000). *Communities of practice*. Cambridge, England: Cambridge University Press.

Elizabeth J. Tisdell, EdD, is professor and coordinator of the graduate programs in adult education at Penn State University—Harrisburg.

Margaret Wojnar, MD, is a pulmonologist, an intensive care physician, and professor at Penn State College of Medicine.

Elizabeth Sinz, MD, is an anesthesiologist, an intensive care physician, a professor, and the associate dean of clinical simulation at the Penn State College of Medicine.

7

The military relies on continuing professional education as a key component to the success of its organization. With decreasing budgets and increasing importance for a force that operates efficiently and thinks critically, the cognitive tension among training, education, and learning comes center stage.

Continuing Professional Education in the Military

Ashley Gleiman, Jeff Zacharakis

Over the past decade, operations in Iraq, Afghanistan, and around the world have demonstrated that U.S. military personnel from all branches (Army, Air Force, Marines, Navy, and Coast Guard) must think critically, communicate well, conduct themselves with integrity and lead others in difficult, ambiguous, and often dangerous situations (U.S. Government Accountability Office [GAO], 2014). To that end, all branches of the military, which fall under the U.S. Department of Defense (USDOD) and U.S. Department of Homeland Security (USDOH) respectively, rely heavily on continuing professional education (CPE) to educate service members throughout their careers, broaden their knowledge, improve performance, and foster collaboration across the ranks and military services (USDOD, 2014; USDOH, 2014; USGAO, 2014).

Currently, the U.S. Department of Defense is one of the largest, most complex organizations in the world (USGAO, 2014), employing more than 3.2 million people (active duty and reserve soldiers, and full-time civilians), and requiring the talents of many professionals including those working in the medical, dental, legal, retail, transportation, financial, construction, shipping, education, space, and of course, defense fields (USDOD, 2014). The multinational and multi-industrial nature of the DOD results in extremely large public organizations with decidedly complex continuing professional education needs. In a sense, CPE within these organizations is the lifeblood that enables personnel participating in programs to acquire and create knowledge.

It should be noted that in the military CPE is a learning process as much as a training opportunity. Whereas earlier research has argued that learning to think critically and understand the complexity of problems is not the primary focus of CPE (Cervero and Daley, 2011; Daley, 2002), in the military this is an essential component even though it may not always be successfully achieved.

NEW DIRECTIONS FOR ADULT AND CONTINUING EDUCATION, no. 151, Fall 2016 © 2016 Wiley Periodicals, Inc.
Published online in Wiley Online Library (wileyonlinelibrary.com) • DOI: 10.1002/ace.20197

According to Dietz and Schroeder (2012), critical thinking requires one to move outside of one's preconceptions and apply processes to a problem that assess and reconstruct the problem in novel ways. In the military, every unit from the smallest platoon to the largest division depends upon its members to know what to do, when to do it, and what factors may lead to success or failure. In contrast to members of other organizations, informed and thinking service men and women are responsible for the lives of their team members and innocent noncombatants. Whether or not CPE strives to increase ethical thinking and problem-solving capacity of its participants is considered to be inherently part of all training and education.

Although the focus of this chapter is on CPE, the term is rarely used within military training and education. In fact, a mixture of terms that includes adult education, professional military education (PME), joint professional military education (JPME), voluntary education (VOLED), continuous learning, continuing education, lifelong learning, organization knowledge, and adult learning are all used interchangeably throughout the U.S. armed forces when referring to CPE (Bohler, 2009; U.S. Department of the Army, 2014; USDOD, 2012; USGAO, 2014). However, for the purpose of this chapter, the term CPE is used throughout when referring to the more common military terms surrounding military education.

In this chapter, we provide a brief historical overview of how CPE has influenced the military, followed by an overview of CPE as a continuum. We then discuss the cognitive tension that exists in the military between the need to train service members for specific tasks, techniques, and procedures and the need to educate service members so they can apply critical thinking skills that are relevant to the environments in which the military operates. We also discuss the dichotomy between training and education. For example, in contrast to other learning environments where training and education may not go hand in hand or have equal importance, military training through repetition is an important component of critical thinking. To emphasize this point, service members are often expected to perform under the pressure and intense adrenaline release during battle or while working in combat zones. Consequently, their reflex action must encompass both understanding the technical aspects of shooting a weapon with deadly force and rational and ethical decision making. Split moment decisions and quick reactions are the norm. There are few other professions that operate under these conditions and are held to the highest standard where the lives of innocents must be protected. Additionally, CPE in the officer corps provides a new dichotomy of whether the focus should remain primarily on procedures and process that strictly benefits the structural needs of the organization, or whether it should focus more on studying historical case studies that broaden one's perspective and provide alternative views on the application of military force. In the latter, learning is achieved by being able to solve complex problems that might not have one correct answer, in contrast to learning how to follow procedures and protocol. Examples such as this highlight how the military in general has addressed

New Directions for Adult and Continuing Education • DOI: 10.1002/ace

this tension. In conclusion, the chapter ends with an overview of the changing landscape of CPE in the military.

Historical CPE Trends

The American armed forces have a long history of offering adult and continuing professional education to its members. Some of the earliest writings from the field of adult education focused on the practice of CPE in the military. These included Houle, Burr, Hamilton, and Yale's (1947). *The Armed Services in Adult Education* and Kidd's (1950) book *Adult Education in Canada* (1950), which focused on the Canadian military and armed forces during World War II. Houle's thinking at this time may have provided the earliest comprehensive argument for CPE in the military, which focused for the most part on building morale. He envisioned that adult education and CPE could be used as a mechanism to foster learning that would strengthen the emotional and intellectual development of service men and women while in the military and be useful once they returned to civilian life. He painted a picture of how CPE can be used during orientation, to share information, and for leader development. Though he did not associate these implications with CPE, he argued that adult education should be introduced through primary associations including place of work to enhance the organization's social structures and loyalty of its personnel and thereby strengthen its war-fighting capacity. This form of emotional intelligence points to the importance for professional education as a social activity within the milieu of the workplace.

At the end of World War II many of the generals and admirals who had led the U.S. military identified the adult and continuing education they received over the course of their career as having played a major role in preparing them for the arduous tasks they confronted during war (W. Murray, 2014). However, almost immediately afterward military colleges began to decline in importance as the pressures of the Cold War and the conduct of major wars in Korea and Vietnam led senior leaders to devalue education in favor of readiness. In other words, these military policy makers believed that all education and training should concentrate on technical aspects required for battle. According to W. Murray (2014), there are two possible explanations to consider when examining this shift. First, senior leaders in the military began to dismiss the idea of offering serious study for their profession, thus believing they were too advanced to be a student after having "learned" everything they needed to know from combat experience. Second, a major reform in the personnel system occurred focusing on the "up or out" industrial organizational model of the time, resulting in a military that created little to no opportunities for broader educational experiences for the service member (W. Murray, 2014).

Following the Vietnam War with the advent of an all-volunteer professional military (as opposed to forced conscription through a draft), the need for a highly skilled military resulted in renewed interest to invest heavily in CPE. Today, in addition to the wide spectrum of on the job training and education programs, for an officer to reach the highest ranks, a graduate degree is often required and noncommissioned officers (NCOs—upper ranks of the enlisted personnel) need at least a bachelor's degree. This professionalization process adheres to the belief that intellectual training through academic coursework strengthens professional soldiers' critical thinking skills, thus enabling them to better solve problems and manage highly technical teams and equipment.

The Continuum of CPE

CPE for all service members in the military exists along a continuum. Along this continuum service personnel have the opportunity to participate in formalized professional education as well as informal learning opportunities throughout their careers in order to broaden their knowledge, improve performance and analytical skills, and be operationally ready for combat at all times. On one side service members experience formalized education opportunities that include professional training and development through many military schools and universities. These opportunities also encompass rote training, memorization, and apprenticeship, which are a large part of how service members learn their craft. In addition there are more informal personal opportunities, such as mentorship, distance learning, and higher education degree-granting programs (Johnson-Freese, 2013). Both levels of professional education opportunities are vital forms of CPE within the context of military education and remain interchangeable throughout one's career.

As broad guidance all military service members experience sequential, yet regularly scheduled periods of formal CPE in the military that are offered based on rank, occupation, service, and organizational needs. However, there is not a one-size-fits-all explanation of how this occurs as it can be vastly different for each individual service member. As a general rule for commissioned officers professional education begins with the precommissioning phase, which is completed at a service academy (U.S. Military Academy, West Point, etc.) or a Reserve Officers Training Corps (ROTC) program at a participating college or university. For NCOs, professional education begins with basic training where service members learn to take orders, trust their leadership, work in teams, and take initiative in the absence of orders followed by advanced technical training related to their military occupation. Over time, military leaders return to the "schoolhouse" every 3 to 5 years during a 20-plus-year career, to engage in learning related to more academic topics including leadership, management theory and practices, military history, operational doctrine, and national defense policy. This extends to technical job specific topics such as nuclear thermodynamics, tactical operations, language application, and intelligence analytics.

Among senior enlisted and commissioned officer ranks in the military, formal CPE is part of the advancement process. Professional military education and specifically joint professional military education (both forms of

New Directions for Adult and Continuing Education • DOI: 10.1002/ace

CPE) serves the purpose of educating service members throughout their careers, broadening their knowledge, improving performance during joint assignments, and eventually fostering collaboration between the different military services (USGAO, 2014). Thus, JPME (joint professional military education) adds incentive to attract officers to joint assignments and possible promotion as a result of the experience. Advanced CPE in the military (professional military education and even JPME) is offered to senior leaders and encompass courses that are intended to provide applicable programs balancing both practical military doctrine and training with academic methodologies that incorporate adult learning principles and promote critical thinking. For example, officers attending a midcareer staff college often come with varying numbers of combat deployments and experiences over the course of their military careers. The experiential element these students bring to the classroom enhances discussions in a variety of contextual matters, further promoting facilitators and students alike to ask the right questions, gain different perspectives, and enable new ways of thinking (Carter, 2010). This process focuses on *how* and not *what* to think, which in turn supports institutional goals in developing officers who are capable of critical thinking and adaptive leadership (Carter, 2010). In this context, the transference of knowledge cannot be directly linked to any single experience in a specific school. It is developed through an accumulation of multiple assignments and schools coupled with more responsibility as one progresses through the ranks.

Although critical thinking is encouraged and fostered in many military institutions, the fundamental and unavoidable limitation of teaching and learning within military education environments revolves around the conservative political nature of the military itself. The military operates within a bureaucratic hierarchy established under a strict chain of command where every member has a direct supervisor. Yet, the military is a highly competitive culture that depends upon cooperative selflessness and teamwork (Carter, 2010). Additionally, this competitive culture is task oriented, which often leaves little tolerance for "grandstanding, prima donnas," or even "all about me" mentalities among the ranks (Carter, 2010).

On the informal end of the CPE continuum, characteristics can include "implicit, unintended, opportunistic and unstructured learning" that fosters the acquisition of knowledge independently of a conscious attempt to learn (Eraut, 2004, p. 250). The contemporary military community tries to foster informal learning as CPE in a number of ways, including experiential learning, mentorship, and more specifically the development of a culture that supports the pursuit of higher education degrees (Bruscino, 2010; Layne, 2008). For example, enlisted military service members who move up in the ranks receive schooling specific to their jobs by way of nondegree-granting programs. This is all part of formal CPE. However, these programs are regularly evaluated by the American Council of Education (ACE) and have college credit that the service member can then use toward a civilian degree program. Although pursuing a civilian degree program is not part of formal

CPE in the military, over time the pursuit of education outside of formal CPE in the military has shown to be vital to personal and professional satisfaction, which in turns promotes performance, and in some cases is required for promotion (Bruscino, 2010). Thus, informal learning opportunities such as higher education at a nonmilitary institution are an integral part of CPE in the military.

Cognitive Tension

Both formal CPE and informal learning opportunities exist in the military to enable service members to develop themselves throughout their career. However, academics, proponents, and critics of CPE within the military suggest that a cognitive tension between training and education continues to exist. Cognitive tension or dissonance comes from holding two conflicting thoughts in the mind at the same time. In a military context, this kind of tension exists for most service members. Yet, the push for critical thinking continues to persist in military academic environments in the context of teamwork and coordination of multiple units with diverse responsibilities.

Within the military, which is heavily bureaucratic and hierarchical, individuals in many different roles and with many different perspectives are in a continual state of dialogue and negotiations. According to Johnson-Freese (2013), the formal academic culture of CPE is intended to promote critical thinking using teaching methodologies that are "associated with understanding a larger context—capabilities achieved through education" (p. 17). Furthermore, many institutions in the military inherently force diverse military and academic cultures to work together and strive to create a healthy tension resulting in a productive learning environment for America's military (Johnson-Freese, 2013).

Within the confines of CPE, the concepts of education and training overlap and are often used interchangeably within the military as both of these terms imply some level of learning and gaining of new knowledge (Carter, 2010). The idea that military education is somehow different from any other form of CPE exists, according to N. Murray (2014), "because of a common conflation of training with education both of which are required as part of the development of a service member" (p. 2). Using the terms interchangeably, according to Murray, is problematic because it is difficult to determine where training (delivery of education) ends and learning (taking up in practice) begins. In reality, education and training (in DOD parlance) differ in that training typically involves teaching and practicing a specific task, skill, or drill in order to operate complicated systems, whereas education teaches the learner a body of knowledge and the opportunity to develop critical thinking skills, which in turn prepares personnel to understand and adapt to complex, dynamic operational environments, (U.S. Air Force, 2006). According to Johnson-Freese (2013), "when training and education are viewed interchangeably, intellectual ability becomes sacrificed to training-friendly metrics" (p. 21) where the focus lies more in delivering content rather than enhancing learning. This is an underlying concern throughout military CPE today.

In military CPE, training often involves right and wrong answers that allow immediate measurement, whereas learning through education is incremental and involves grappling with ambiguity (Johnson-Freese, 2013). Although there is truth in these constructs, the relationship among education, learning, and training is far more complex and intimately intertwined mostly due to entrenched cultural aspects within the military. Generally speaking, CPE within the military invokes a process-oriented mentality, which is imperative to help keep service members and noncombatants alive in high-risk operational situations. According to Johnson-Freese (2013), personnel may be well trained and strong leaders, but neither characteristic equates to being broadly educated or having the ability to think critically. To think critically, one must move outside of "preconceptions and apply processes to a problem that assess and reconstructs the problem in novel ways" (Dietz & Schroeder, 2012, p. 30). However, critical thinking is also an inherently political process controlled by the dominant discourse, which muddies the waters for how it is achieved.

A perfect example of the cognitive tension between education and training in the U.S. military is a case study of the School of Advanced Military Studies (SAMS) curriculum from 2008 to 2013. SAMS is an elite part of CPE in the United States Army. In SAMS, the Army selects midcareer officers for the 1-year intense academic program in tactics, operations, and strategy based upon merit. Graduates of the program go on to serve as operational planners in high-level military staffs and are charged with creating war plans for military operations. In 2008, after the war plans failed to bring about a clear victory in Iraq, the director of SAMS determined that the curriculum was too process focused and did not provide for the critical and creative thinking necessary to address military operations in complex environments (Banach & Ryan, 2009). From 2008 to 2010, the curriculum was changed to incorporate design methodology. The results were mixed. Although many in the military community praised the design curriculum and its broad, nonsequential methodology, others complained that the curriculum was too esoteric and that the lack of process contributed to military plans that were simply not executable by the hierarchical and bureaucratic military organizations. Struck by the manifestation of this cognitive tension, the subsequent director of SAMS decided to rebalance the curriculum. Though this SAMS director did not eliminate the design curriculum or the methodology, design, and other more process-oriented systems were incorporated into "integrated planning" to leverage critical and creative thinking or design, while ensuring that SAMS graduates could still write military plans that are executable (Grigsby et al., 2011). The cognitive tension between training for process-oriented thinking and educating to understand complex problems continues to manifest itself in the SAMS curriculum to this day.

According to Zacharakis and Van Der Werff (2012), the military's goal today is to encourage its leaders at all levels to think critically, but not *too critically* as this could possibly lead to questioning ideologies within the military structure. For example, on July 16, 2012 General Dempsey (2012), chairman of the Joint Chiefs of Staff, issued a Joint White Paper in which he emphasized the purpose of PME was to "develop leaders by conveying a broad body of professional knowledge and developing the habits of mind essential to our profession" (p. 1). Conversely, the general approach to teaching critical thinking skills in the military today primarily focuses on targeting higher ranking enlisted and officers as opposed to younger (and lower ranking) service members (Zacharakis & Van Der Werff, 2012). Overall, this contradiction of vision and reality surrounding PME is where many educators today believe CPE in the military fails the service member (Johnson-Freese, 2013; Zacharakis & Van Der Werff, 2012). On one hand, the military as an organization promotes critical thinking, learning, and adaptive leadership through education. On the other, it promotes authority, hegemony, and cultural tradition through training. The juxtaposition of these two ideals is where cognitive tension exists and where the military operates today.

The Changing Landscape

Today, debate around CPE continues within military circles (N. Murray, 2014). Between 2007 and 2011, large DOD budgets and the growing needs for additional research led to the expansion of many CPE programs within the military (USGAO, 2014). However, following a decade of war, new budget restrictions have resulted in downsizing or eliminating some CPE programs in the military, leading to a growing reliance on civilian institutions and partnerships to fill the need for education and research.

Although General Dempsey (2013) articulated that education is "one of [the] top priorities in developing the Joint Force 2020" (p. 1), the reality is that military leaders will adjust priorities and budgets that potentially will defund or eliminate many CPE opportunities for service members (Barnes, 2014). According to Johnson-Freese (2015), military CPE "needs to be fixed" (p. 1). The fear is that with budget cuts the tension that exists between training and education will become one sided and fiscal concerns will trump the goal of critical thinking through education (Johnson-Freese, 2015). The current CPE system continues to be under review, and this review offers the perfect arena where military leaders can prioritize opportunities to address current educational shortcomings (Barnes, 2014). Hence, today's major challenges are twofold—the first challenge is to achieve organizational buy-in despite cultural differences among the military forces, and the second is to balance education and learning with operational readiness and fiscal uncertainty. To implement these recommendations will require each military service to accept CPE's usefulness in sustaining leader development and mission readiness.

Conclusion

CPE within the military is an essential component in educating and training service members and leaders who can think critically and adapt quickly in changing environments. Historical influences from adult education have and continue to shape how CPE is developed in the military. However, the gap between critical thinking, expertise, and CPE is not going to go away in the military because it is difficult to change the cultural physics, budget constraints, and hierarchical nature of the situation. According to Bruscino (2010), "The nature of war is such that as they move up the ranks, service members shift emphasis from tactics to operations to strategy to advising military and national policy, without ever losing the need to keep an understanding of the other levels" (p. 145). How a military force will continue to do this falls in line with the *less is more* mentality faced today in times of economic uncertainty.

Overall, CPE in the military today is formal education that according to critics lacks potential critical thinking development. With changes in leadership and the constant flux of perceptions surrounding CPE in the military, one thing is certain: Informal education training and opportunities through academic programs are where the slack can possibly be quickened.

References

Banach, S., & Ryan, A. (2009, March–April). The art of design: A design methodology. *Military Review*, 105–115.

Barnes, S. W. (2014). *21 century military-media relationships: Improving relations and the narrative through education*. Norfolk, VA: Joint Forces Staff College, National Defense University. Retrieved from http://www.dtic.mil/get-tr-doc/pdf?AD=ADA600209

Bohler, J. A. (2009). *Education technology impact on Department of Defense financial manager continuing professional education programs* (Doctoral dissertation). Available from ProQuest Dissertations & Theses Full Text. (Order No. 3386180). Retrieved from http://search.proquest.com.er.lib.k-state.edu/docview/304829737?accountid=11789

Bruscino, T. (2010). Navel gazing Google deep: The expertise gap in the academic-military relationship. In D. Higbee (Ed.), *Military culture and education* (pp. 139–148). Burlington, VT: Ashgate.

Carter, B. L. (2010). No "holidays from history": Adult learning, professional military education, and teaching history. In D. Higbee (Ed.), *Military culture and education* (pp. 167–182). Burlington, VT: Ashgate.

Cervero R. M., & Daley, B. J. (2011). Continuing professional education: Multiple stakeholders and agendas. In K. Rubenson (Ed.), *Adult learning and education* (pp. 140–145). Oxford, UK: Elsevier.

Daley, B. J. (2002). Continuing professional education: Creating the future. *Adult Learning, 13*, 15–17. doi:10.1177/104515950201300406

Dempsey, M. E. (2012, July 16). Joint education white paper. Retrieved from http://www.dtic.mil/doctrine/concepts/white_papers/cjcs_wp_education.pdf

Dempsey, M. E. (2013, June 28). Desired leader attributes for joint force 2020. Retrieved from https://jdeis.js.mil/jdeis/jel/education/cm_0166_13.pdf

Dietz, A. S., & Schroeder, E. A. (2012). Integrating critical thinking in the U.S. Army: Decision support red teams. In J. Zacharakis & C. Polson (Eds.), *New Directions for Adult and Continuing Education: No. 136. Beyond training: The rise of adult education in the military* (pp. 29–40). San Francisco, CA: Jossey-Bass.

Eraut, M. (2004). Informal learning in the workplace. *Studies in Continuing Education, 26*(2), 247–273). doi:10.1080/158037042000225245

Grigsby, W. W., Gorman, S., Marr, J., McLamb, J., Stewart, M., & Schifferle, P. (2011, January–February). Integrated planning: The operations process, design, and the military decision making process. *Military Review*, 28–35.

Houle, C. O., Burr, E. W., Hamilton, T. H., & Yale, J. R. (1947). *The armed services and adult education.* Washington, DC: American Council on Education.

Johnson-Freese, J. (2013). *Educating America's military.* New York, NY: Routledge.

Johnson-Freese, J. (2015, May 7). *Educating the U.S. military: Is real change possible?* Retrieved from http://warontherocks.com/2015/05/educating-the-u-s-military-is-real-change-possible/

Kidd, J. R. (1950). *Adult education in Canada.* Toronto: Canadian Association for Adult Education.

Layne, L. L. (2008). *Military leadership: Encouraging enlisted personnel to participate in continuing education (Order No. 3349274).* Available from ProQuest Dissertations & Theses Full Text. (304353585). Retrieved from http://search.proquest.com.er.lib.k-state.edu/docview/304353585?accountid=11789

Murray, N. (2014, July 29). *More dissent needed: Critical thinking and PME.* Retrieved from http://warontherocks.com/2014/07/more-dissent-needed-critical-thinking-and-pme/

Murray, W. (2014). Is professional military education necessary? *Navy War College Review, 67*(1), 145.

U.S. Air Force. (2006). *Leadership and force development: Air Force doctrine document 1-1.* Retrieved from https://doctrine.af.mil/download.jsp?filename=Volume-2-Leadership.pdf

U.S. Department of the Army. (2014). *Army FY15 budget overview.* Retrieved from http://www.defenseinnovationmarketplace.mil/resources/ArmyFY2015Budgetoverview.pdf

U.S. Department of Defense. (2012). *Enlisted professional military education policy 1805.1.* Washington, DC: U.S. Government Printing Office.

U.S. Department of Defense. (2014). *About the Department of Defense (DOD).* Retrieved from http://www.defense.gov/about/

U.S. Department of Homeland Security. (2014). About the Department of Homeland Security. Retrieved from http://www.dhs.gov/about-dhs

U.S. Government Accountability Office. (2014). *Joint professional military education: Opportunities exist for greater oversight and coordination of associated research institutions. Congressional Report.* Retrieved from http://www.dtic.mil/get-tr-doc/pdf?AD=ADA595905

Zacharakis, J., & Van Der Werff, J. (2012). The future of adult education in the military. In J. Zacharakis & C. Polson (Eds.), *New Directions for Adult and Continuing Education: No. 136. Beyond training: The rise of adult education in the military* (pp. 89–98). San Francisco, CA: Jossey-Bass.

ASHLEY GLEIMAN, PhD, is an editorial assistant for Adult Education Quarterly and an education coordinator for American Public University System.

JEFF ZACHARAKIS, EdD, is a professor of adult education in the Department of Educational Leadership, Kansas State University.

New Directions for Adult and Continuing Education • DOI: 10.1002/ace

This chapter synthesizes the main themes in the issue in an overall update from the field of current CPE thinking and practice.

Continuing Professional Education: Enduring Challenges, New Developments, and Future Vistas

Maureen J. Coady

The purpose of this volume is to initiate a critical analysis and discussion of the current "state of the field" thinking about continuing professional education (CPE). Much like Mott and Daley's (2000) work, the intent is to revisit and update practitioners on CPE trends, issues, and practices across a variety of contexts and to highlight new thinking and developments in practice to assist them in setting new directions for CPE. In this chapter, I review the terrain covered in each chapter, and I offer some general insights for the future.

As the chapters in this volume reveal, history matters. Debates about CPE, what it is for, and how it might be conceptualized, have been ongoing for 50 years and have been continued by the contributors to this issue. A process of taking stock reveals that almost 40 years after the publication of *Continuous Learning in the Professions* (Houle, 1980), many of the challenges identified by Houle and also by Cervero (2000) and Mott and Daley (2000) persist today as focal points for change. Despite Houle's caution not to focus on increasing the number of formal educational offerings, as well as Daley and Mott's (2000) vision of CPE providers as facilitators of learning, and the significant consensus on how professionals learn, most professional development and CPE practices continue to focus on delivering content rather than on enhancing learning. A unifying picture of effective CPE across professional groups remains elusive, and continuing education serves increasingly to regulate practice and to allow for the relicensure of professionals. We have not come as far as Houle thought we might.

Clearly, the persistent issue identified by Cervero in 2000—multiple stakeholders with diverse competing professional, social, institutional, and educational agendas—remains the key stumbling block. The critical questions he raised then—*Continuing education for what?* (the struggle between updating professionals' knowledge versus improving practice), *Who benefits from*

NEW DIRECTIONS FOR ADULT AND CONTINUING EDUCATION, no. 151, Fall 2016 © 2016 Wiley Periodicals, Inc.
Published online in Wiley Online Library (wileyonlinelibrary.com) • DOI: 10.1002/ace.20198

continuing education? (the struggle for turf versus collaborative relationships), and *Who will provide continuing education?*—remain relevant. Acknowledging the growth of CPE in organizations and workplaces, Jeris and Conway (2003) added a fourth question to Cervero's list: *What impact does the workplace as the site for CPE have on its planning, design, delivery, content and participation, and outcomes?* (the struggle between continuing education's learning agenda and the goal of performance improvement through increased productivity). On the one hand, the lack of significant progress in CPE can be seen as a resistance to growth in the profession and, on the other hand, it can be seen as providing a line of inquiry that can be used for clarification and consensus on a more integrated approach to CPE.

As Cervero and Daley (Cervero & Daley, 2011; Daley & Cervero, 2015) have considered and consistently pointed out, including in their Chapter 1, building an effective systems of CPE is a complex and long-term political process that will involve continued bargaining and negotiation not only among providers but within the wider social, professional, institutional, and educational agendas that are the contested spaces of CPE. Meanwhile, the extensive body of knowledge and insights on the importance of learning in CPE can be used to inform those negotiations so that a more integrated approach to CPE can be achieved.

As is apparent in this issue, despite enduring challenges, educational scholars continue their investigations, and have made considerable progress. This volume updates the field and also offers many promising new conceptual insights and frameworks for thinking about CPE practice. Educational scholars, embracing the importance of lifelong professional learning and education, have played a key role in the development of CPE. The ever-emerging scholarship of Mott and Daley (2000), Cervero (2000, 2001), Cervero and Wilson (2000, 2006), and others in and beyond this volume continues to engage professionals from the field, significantly deepening the conceptual understanding of the experience of continuous professional learning and also the nature of professional knowledge and how it is constructed and reconstructed through different types of learning transitions and contexts. Overall, the collective works of many CPE scholars reinforce the notion that professional knowledge is embodied, contextual, and embedded in practice. An increase in learning occurs through practice, experience, and critically reflective action within contexts that may, and usually do, pose dilemmas, and continuous professional learning is situated, social, and constructed through and in practice.

There are also significant new insights in this issue that build on earlier conceptual thinking about professional learning and CPE practice. In Chapter 1, Daley and Cervero advance Daley's (2000) earlier thinking on constructivist learning by acknowledging that a professional's identity is deeply intertwined with the processes of developing and sustaining knowledge in practice. They concur with others (e.g., Dirkx, Gilley, & Maycunich-Gilley, 2004) that professional development knowledge is influenced by the many subjective and richly felt (embodied) dimensions of practice, including the self and web of relationships, feelings, emotions, and instincts that shape professionals. Cervero and Daley and later Bierema (Chapter 5) support the notion that lifelong learning in professional practice is characterized by an evolving critical awareness of the self in relationship with itself, with others, and with its social and cultural context. As such, self-understanding can serve as a major aim of continuing professional development and CPE practice.

A concern for constructivist learning and a learning-focused approach to CPE is apparent elsewhere in this volume and extends from conceptual thinking to CPE practice strategies. Hansman, in Chapter 3, for example, profiles how mentoring relationships (both formal and informal) can foster many different types of learning, including critical reflection and critical coconstruction of knowledge. Reflecting critically and unpacking learning events or activities though discourse aids mentors and mentees in understanding the unique needs of those involved in a mentoring relationship. A critical-constructivist perspective enables the conversation to extend to the power mentors have—acknowledged or unacknowledged—over mentees, and can foster dialogue that can transform the relationship to one where mentors and mentees share power. Hansman contends that such constructive dialogues, whether constituted as dyadic or group reflection, can also transform the organizational status quo and encourage a bottom-up culture of learning in organizations that are driven by the real and urgent needs of professionals. She provides helpful examples of empowering mentoring relationships where power differentials were mitigated by collaboratively planning ways to share knowledge and engage in experiential learning.

Cranton (Chapter 4), in her exploration of CPE for teachers and university and college faculty, contends that learning in CPE relies on a collaborative environment where participants exchange ideas and socially construct knowledge of the profession. According to Cranton, colearning, emancipatory learning, experiential learning, and socially constructed learning all involve sharing power; the facilitator builds on what participants know and becomes a colearner in the process. Yet, despite the immediate advantages of informal or nonformal learning while doing, Cranton observes that teachers often turn to formal learning and instrumental knowledge to comprehensively improve their practice. She argues that teachers, and CPE for teachers, need to be concerned with the development of communicative and emancipatory knowledge that helps teachers to be socially aware, self-determining, and self-reflective. In the context of online learning, where most CPE for teachers occurs, she offers strategies (e.g., self-awareness exercises, critical reflection, sharing stories, and discussing authenticity in teaching) to foster the development of communicative and emancipatory knowledge, and potentially transformative learning.

Bierema, writing on CPE in organizations and workplaces in Chapter 5, connects with Mott and Daley's (2000) earlier vision that the business of CPE should be:

The identification of problems in professional's practice and the determination of how education can foster professional development programs that ultimately promote the ability to work in the uncertain, confusing and dynamic world of professional practice for the betterment of clients. (p. 81)

Bierema is identifying the fluidity of life for highly interdependent and interconnected professionals who struggle to keep pace with relentless change and unpredictable outcomes. Coping, she contends, involves constantly being ready to change and adapt in order to stay current with technology, respond to regulations, and stay relevant within a globally competitive context. Bierema offers an alternative conceptualization of professional learning and development that can be used as a basis for planning CPE that is more relevant in complex organizational and workplace contexts and that can help professionals to cope with ambiguity, expand their capacity to make meaning, and take timely action under conditions of uncertainty.

Like the teachers Cranton writes about in Chapter 4, Tisdell, Wojnar, and Sinz (Chapter 6) highlight the complex situation that is created when learning for CPE is related to a discipline operating independent of learning about teaching. Tisdell et al. highlight this dual challenge that occurs for medical professionals who try to keep pace with the disciplinary knowledge base while also needing to learn about clinical teaching simultaneously. They draw on the more recent work of Cervero and Wilson (2006) who described how a program and curriculum can be developed in response to a specific CPE need identified through process of collaborative dialogue and an expanding knowledge of each other's contexts and needs. For example, Tisdell et al. describe how they used this process to develop a Graduate Certificate in Adult Education in the Health and Medical Professions within a state college of medicine. The model that Cervero and Wilson proposed for negotiating power and interests for curriculum development is innovative and has wide appeal in other contexts and lends itself conceptually to negotiating the wider challenges and contested spaces within CPE that have been so enduring. Like other chapter, writers, including Cranton, Hansman, and Bierema, Tisdell et al. observe the growing concern with interprofessional teamwork and counter that this process of collaborative dialogue including communities of practice (Wenger, 1998) can support problem solving leading to the development of strong interprofessional and multidisciplinary competencies and teams and potentially to organizational transformation.

Finally, Gleiman and Zacharakis in Chapter 7 highlight historical trends and shifting support for CPE in the military as well as an enduring emphasis in military education on continuous member development and the integration of adult learning principles in military education to foster higher order thinking skills. Such higher order or critical thinking skills enable members to work in dynamic and often ambiguous operational environments and to understand their individual role and responsibilities within the overall mission of the military unit and/or organization. In this context, cognitive tension is observed as members think critically within a hierarchical and bureaucratic military organization, where thinking *too critically* can be perceived as questioning ideologies within the military structure. Similar to the workers described by Bierema in Chapter 5, members of the military at all levels must cope with great ambiguity. Yet, the military lays claim to human capital as embodied in their members as their most valuable asset and invests accordingly in adult education for individual growth, maturity, and learning in order to achieve the collective goals of the organization. Clearly, there are unique challenges for CPE in the military but also lessons to be learned from their considerable commitment to human capital development that have application elsewhere.

In sum, the authors all appear to lament the dwindling progress with CPE; yet all identify areas that could be explored further. The field can be heartened by this enduring interest in the future and consoled that there are emerging scholars who want to bring the field further and to advance a model of learning at the heart of CPE practice. Houle's (1980) vision of moving beyond counting courses and programs is being fulfilled, if this volume is any indication. As professions evolve, and their learning needs become more complex, there will be CPE researchers and practitioners to investigate further. Houle would be pleased.

References

Cervero, R. M. (2000). Trends and issues in continuing professional education. In B. J. Daley & V. W. Mott (Eds.), *New Directions for Adult and Continuing Education: No. 86. Charting a course for continuing professional education* (pp. 3–12). San Francisco, CA: Jossey-Bass.

Cervero, R. M. (2001). Continuing professional education in transition, 1981–2000. *International Journal of Lifelong Learning, 20*(1–2), 16–30.

Cervero R. M., & Daley, B. J. (2011). Continuing professional education: Multiple stakeholders and agendas. In K. Rubenson (Ed.), *Adult learning and education* (pp. 140–145). Oxford, UK: Elsevier.

Cervero, R. M., & Wilson, A. L. (2000). *Power in practice: Adult education and the struggle for knowledge and power in society.* San Francisco, CA: Jossey-Bass.

Cervero, R. M., & Wilson, A. L. (2006). *Working the planning table: Negotiating democratically for adult continuing and workplace education.* San Francisco, CA: Jossey-Bass.

Daley, B. J. (2000). Learning in professional practice. In V. W. Mott & B. J. Daley (Eds.), *New Directions for Adult and Continuing Education: No. 86. Charting a course for continuing professional education* (pp. 33–43). San Francisco, CA: Jossey-Bass.

Daley, B. J., & Mott, V. W. (2000). Continuing professional education: From vision to reality. In B. J. Daley & V. W. Mott (Eds.), *New Directions for Adult and Continuing Education: No. 86. Charting a course for continuing professional education* (pp. 80–85). San Francisco, CA: Jossey-Bass.

Daley, B. J., & Cervero, R. M. (2015). Continuing professional education, development and learning. In R. Poell, T. Rocco, & G. Roth (Eds.), *The Routledge companion to human resource development* (pp. 40–49). New York, NY: Routledge, Taylor and Francis.

Dirkx, J., Gilley, J. W., & Maycunich-Gilley, A. (2004). Change theory in CPE and HRD: Toward a holistic view of learning and change in work. *Advances in Developing Human Resources, 6*(1), 35–51. doi:10.1177/1523422303260825

Houle, C. O. (1980). *Continuing learning in the professions.* San Francisco, CA: Jossey-Bass.

Jeris, L. H., & Conway, A. E. (2003). Time to regrade the terrain of continuing professional education: Views from practitioners. *Adult Learning*, *14*(1), 34–36. doi:10.1177/104515950301400110

Mott, V. W., & Daley, B. J. (Eds.). (2000). *New Directions for Adult and Continuing Education: No. 86. Charting a course for continuing professional education*. San Francisco, CA: Jossey-Bass.

Wenger, E. (1998). *Communities of practice: Learning, meaning, and identity*. New York, NY: Cambridge University Press.

MAUREEN COADY *is an associate professor and the chair of the Department of Adult Education at Saint Francis Xavier University, Antigonish, Nova Scotia, Canada.*

Index

Abdullah, K. L., 57
Academic vice presidents (AVP), 72
Accreditation Council for Graduate Medical Education (ACGME), 73
Adult Education in Canada, 83
Adult Education Research Conference (2014), 77
Ainley, P., 61
Alegre, J., 63
American Board of Internal Medicine, 13
American Board of Medical Specialties (ABMS), 13
American Council of Education (ACE), 85
American Counseling Association: supporting professional identity, 38–39
American Heart Association, 76
The Armed Services in Adult Education, 83
Association of American Medical Colleges (AAMC), 72
Azzaretto, J. F., 10

Balan, D., 55
Banach, S., 87
Barnes, S. W., 88
Bauer, M., 56
Baumgartner, L., 23
Benner, P., 20, 25, 26, 27, 60
Bierema, L. L., 6, 53, 55, 61, 67, 94, 95
Bohler, J. A., 82
Bolman, L., 24, 25
Bortner, T., 77
Boud, D., 20, 22
Brandt, B., 15
Brockett, M., 56
Brookfield, S., 27, 35
Brookfield, S. S., 46
Brooks, A., 27
Brooks, A. K., 63
Bruscino, T., 85, 86, 89
Burr, E. W., 83

Caffarella, R., 70
Carter, B. L., 85, 86
Cervero, R., 11, 16, 19, 20, 21, 24, 27, 31, 32, 35, 36, 56, 57, 69, 71, 72
Cervero, R. M., 6, 9–13, 15–18, 19, 29, 55, 56, 57, 62, 81, 91–94

Charness, N., 25
Chiva, R., 63
Chong, M. C., 57
Clark, C., 32
Clark, E., 55, 57, 61
Clyde, N. J., 57
Coady, M., 22, 69
Coady, M. J., 91, 96
Colbert, S., 31
Colley, H., 32
Communicative knowledge, 44–45, 46
Complementary and alternative medicine (CAM), 12
Constructivist learning theory, 22–23. *See also* Continuing professional education (CPE)
Conti, G. J., 55
Continuing education (CE), 12
Continuing education units (CEU), 69
Continuing professional development credit (CPD), 37
Continuing professional education (CPE), 9; background and historical perspectives, 10–11; boundary-crossing cognitive, 62–63; challenges, new developments and future prospects of, 91–95; colearning online, 48–49; contested spaces of, 12–16; contextual sensitivity, 61–62; critical-constructivist perspective, 36; critiques of, 55–57; cultural knowledge, 60–61; curriculum development, 71–73; defined, 31, 54–55; developing professional practice, 25–26; and discipline depth, 58–59; educational agendas, 15–16; education, power, and responsibility, 76–77; expanded model of learning in, 20–21; fostering, 49–51; generative, 64–65; graduate certificate and master's program, 73–75; implications for the provision of, 26–27; inadequate, 57; innovative mentoring relationship, 36–37; institutional agendas, 13; interpersonal and organizational skills, 62–63; and interprofessional team, 73; knowledge construction for professional practice, 22–25; learning in, 33; learning

97

NEW DIRECTIONS FOR ADULT AND CONTINUING EDUCATION
ORDER FORM SUBSCRIPTION AND SINGLE ISSUES

DISCOUNTED BACK ISSUES:

Use this form to receive 20% off all back issues of *New Directions for Adult and Continuing Education*.
All single issues priced at **$23.20** (normally $29.00)

TITLE	ISSUE NO.	ISBN

Call 1-800-835-6770 or see mailing instructions below. When calling, mention the promotional code JBNND to receive your discount. For a complete list of issues, please visit www.wiley.com/WileyCDA/WileyTitle/productCd-ACE.html

SUBSCRIPTIONS: (1 YEAR, 4 ISSUES)

☐ New Order   ☐ Renewal

U.S.	☐ Individual: $89	☐ Institutional: $356
CANADA/MEXICO	☐ Individual: $89	☐ Institutional: $398
ALL OTHERS	☐ Individual: $113	☐ Institutional: $434

Call 1-800-835-6770 or see mailing and pricing instructions below.
Online subscriptions are available at www.onlinelibrary.wiley.com

ORDER TOTALS:

Issue / Subscription Amount: $ _____

Shipping Amount: $ _____
(for single issues only – subscription prices include shipping)

Total Amount: $ _____

SHIPPING CHARGES:

First Item $6.00
Each Add'l Item $2.00

(No sales tax for U.S. subscriptions. Canadian residents, add GST for subscription orders. Individual rate subscriptions must be paid by personal check or credit card. Individual rate subscriptions may not be resold as library copies.)

BILLING & SHIPPING INFORMATION:

☐ **PAYMENT ENCLOSED:** *(U.S. check or money order only. All payments must be in U.S. dollars.)*

☐ **CREDIT CARD:** ☐ VISA   ☐ MC   ☐ AMEX

Card number _____Exp. Date_____

Card Holder Name_____Card Issue #_____

Signature _____Day Phone_____

☐ **BILL ME:** *(U.S. institutional orders only. Purchase order required.)*

Purchase order # _____
Federal Tax ID 13559302 • GST 89102-8052

Name_____

Address_____

Phone_____ E-mail_____

Copy or detach page and send to: **John Wiley & Sons, Inc. / Jossey Bass**
PO Box 55381
Boston, MA 02205-9850

PROMO JBNND

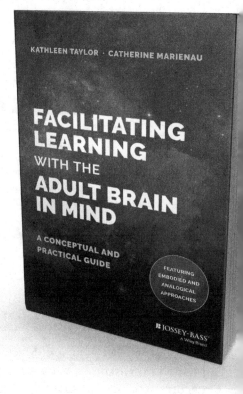

Printed in the United States
By Bookmasters